SACRED PATHS
FOR
MODERN MEN

To Write to the Author

If you wish to contact the author or would like more information about this book, please write to the author in care of Llewellyn Worldwide and we will forward your request. Both the author and publisher appreciate hearing from you and learning of your enjoyment of this book and how it has helped you. Llewellyn Worldwide cannot guarantee that every letter written to the author can be answered, but all will be forwarded. Please write to:

Dagonet Dewr
℅ Llewellyn Worldwide
2143 Wooddale Drive, Dept. 978-0-7387-1252-9
Woodbury, MN 55125-2989, U. S. A.

Please enclose a self-addressed stamped envelope for reply,
or $1.00 to cover costs. If outside the USA, enclose an
international postal reply coupon.

Many of Llewellyn's authors have websites with additional information and resources. For more information, please visit our website at www.llewellyn.com.

SACRED PATHS
FOR
MODERN MEN
A WAKE UP CALL FROM YOUR 12 ARCHETYPES

DAGONET DEWR

Llewellyn Publications
Woodbury, Minnesota

First Edition
Second Printing, 2018

Book design by Steffani Sawyer
Cover art © 2007 by David Wasserman/Brand X Pictures/PunchStock
Cover design by Ellen Dahl
Editing by Brett Fechheimer
Llewellyn is a registered trademark of Llewellyn Worldwide, Ltd.

Library of Congress Cataloging-in-Publication Data
Dewr, Dagonet, 1968–
  Sacred paths for modern men : a wake up call from your 12 archetypes /
Dagonet Dewr — 1st ed.
      p.   cm.
  Includes bibliographical references.
  ISBN 978-0-7387-1252-9
  1. Men—Religious life. 2. Neopaganism. I. Title.
  BL625.65.D49 2007
  299'.94—dc22
                          2007037822

Llewellyn Publications
A Division of Llewellyn Worldwide, Ltd.
2143 Wooddale Drive, Dept. 978-0-7387-1252-9
Woodbury, Minnesota 55125-2989, U.S.A.
www.llewellyn.com

Printed in the United States of America

CONTENTS

INTRODUCTION

During the four years I was the managing editor of *new-Witch* magazine, my professional life was fraught with joys, sorrows, and some things that can only be classified as annoyances. I dealt with all of them in turn, but I must admit that one of them really, really toasted my marshmallows—mostly because it was avoidable with just a bit of research and common sense.

I've had it happen time and time again. I'm sorting my way through my e-mail and there it is. Three words that fill my heart with cynicism: "Dear Miss Dewr."

I've checked, really I have. My caricature on the *newWitch* editorial page, while somewhat cartoonish, seemed to me recognizably male. I have been listed as male in every interview, article, and book I've appeared in that worried about my gender. My biography on the Pagan Pride Project website is pretty clear. To the best of my knowledge, the only time I have appeared in drag in public was Halloween 1995, but that was almost twelve years ago, for Goddess' sake. (And I don't think anyone has any pictures left. I bought them all.) Yet every so often—in fact, if I had to make an unscientific guess, about one communication out of ten—it is assumed I'm female.

All jokes aside, the question remains: why?

As much as I hate to say it, I fear that it's some sort of unconscious sexism. Despite the examples of Gerald Gardner, Isaac Bonewits, Skip Ellison, Scott Cunningham, Oberon Zell-Ravenheart, Steve Foster, Stewart Farrar, Christopher Penczak, Kerr Cuhulain, Brian Ewing, Victor Anderson, Drake Spaeth, Gavin Bone, Raven Grimassi, Bill Kilborn, and so many others, to some people the default gender for Pagan leadership—and perhaps even Pagan belief—is female. There's some filter that's grown up around what we think about our work that says Pagans—and especially witches—just aren't male.

This book isn't about that. (Maybe someday I'll write that book. Then again, maybe I'm just hypersensitive to people misaddressing communication to me. Get back to me on that.) But the subject got me thinking about what this book *is* about—male mysticism. Male magick. Male gods. Male prayer. Male faith. Maybe the gender assumption comes from the fact that as men, we don't talk about our faith, our beliefs, the moments when we pray and sing and hope, the moments when we feel our gods close to us, their hands on our shoulders, our Blessed Dead standing behind us.

It's a cliché that's sadly true: we men don't talk about our feelings very well. And religious faith, religious passion, the fervent desire to change and shape the world—the craft of the Witch—is a feeling, and a deep, miraculous one at that. We have our own version of Maiden, Mother, and Crone; we have our own archetypes that resonate down the trail of the centuries. We have our own symbols, deep currents of the unconscious and the shared consciousness. We come from a long woven cord of men who worshiped their gods before we lost touch with the numinosity of the world around us.

For my own part, I had several things that led me back to my sacred nature as a man. I had children, and that made a difference. I went through loss: I lost both of my parents at an early age. But I was quite an emotional and personal mess when, in 2001, I started attending therapy with a man by the name of Ed.

I'd picked Ed out of a list of therapists at random—he turned out to be a retired Methodist minister and a gentle, soft-spoken, grandfatherly man. However, he could—and did—kick my ass when necessary. He was an elder in a group called the ManKind Project (www.mkp.org), a group that puts on a weekend called the New Warrior Training Adventure. After three years with Ed, I attended that weekend in April of 2004—and I rediscovered my own sacred masculine. The NWTA is the single greatest thing I ever did. I regained my ability to walk my path in integrity and accountability.

My goal became to bring that energy to all men, with a special focus on bringing that energy to the Pagan community. What I want is for all men to regain their own ability to walk our sacred paths. We may not all call it the same thing, but the symbols are powerful and transcend individual differences. *Sacred Paths for Modern Men* is about those symbols, those archetypes of the Divine Masculine. Specifically, this book is about using those symbols and archetypes to achieve greater understanding of ourselves, and through that to become more aware, more functional, and more enlightened in our everyday role as men.

As men we will experience the Divine Masculine through prayer, lore, magickal workings, meditation, and personal experience, and I hope that this work provides some guidance and illumination as part of that process. I hope women who walk with us through this journey, getting in touch with their animus as we have tried to reach our anima, will get something out of this work as well. Finally, I hope that this book encourages all of you to walk this road with me, and to see God—some god—in the face of every man you meet, every day.

I want to give credit where credit is due. There have been many inspirations on this road, and I can't mention them all—but I'll sure try.

To my coven of thirteen years, Thalia Clan—what can I say? So many of these discoveries I made with all of you. Keep the stories alive.

To writers who have influenced my thoughts on masculinity and spirituality—including Robert Moore and Douglas Gillette, Scott Cunningham, Tom Cowan, Isaac Bonewits, Robert Heinlein, James Carse, Richard Bach, Robert M. Pirsig, Guy Gavriel Kay, and many others—I am a small man standing on the shoulder of giants.

To my brother New Warriors in the ManKind Project, and especially to the Spirit Quest I-Group in the Indiana community and the Imperfect I-Group in the Austin community: someone saved my life tonight and it was all of you. I hope to pay it forward for the rest of my life. Love you guys.

To my father, Patrick Linn, and my son, Corwin Patrick—I love you both.

To my daughters, Aven and Catrien—be great women as your father has tried to be a good man.

And to Elisabeth, who has been the soul of patience while I wasted too much time—you are, indeed, the wind at my back.

I

MAPPING OUT THE JOURNEY

God created man in His own image, and man, being a gentleman, returned the favor.

—Mark Twain

So. What the heck is a god anyway? My speech coach always counseled me to define my terms early in the work before I confused people. We all have our own definitions, especially so with emotionally charged terms—and the Divine is about as emotionally charged as it gets. Nevertheless, let's take a crack at a definition and see what we get.

In a rhetorical tactic that would bring joy to the heart of my third-grade teacher, Ms. Kotek, let's start with a dictionary definition[1]:

god (*n.*)

1. A being conceived as the perfect, omnipotent, omniscient originator and ruler of the Universe, the principal object of faith and worship in monotheistic religions. The force, effect, or a manifestation or aspect of this being.

2. A being of supernatural powers or attributes, believed in and worshiped by a people, especially a male deity thought to control some part of nature or reality.

---

1. "god." Dictionary.com. Reprinted from *The American Heritage® Dictionary of the English Language, Fourth Edition*. (Boston: Houghton Mifflin, 2004). http://dictionary.reference.com/browse/god (accessed May 29, 2007).

3. An image of a supernatural being; an idol.

4. One that is worshiped, idealized, or followed: *Money was their god*.

5. A very handsome man.

6. A powerful ruler or despot.

So how, as men and as Pagans, do we define the term "god"? That's not an easy one to call out. For starters, we immediately hit the problem of defining "Pagan"—and that discussion could take over this manuscript faster than kudzu eating your front lawn. (To paraphrase the great Alton Brown: "That's another book.") There is also the consideration that this book isn't just for Pagans, though I am certainly writing it from a Pagan viewpoint; for that reason, we need a definition with some flexibility and some utilitarianism.

If we look at the definition above, though, we can probably work on it a little until it fits our purposes—rather like someone might customize a car, or a software load.

For starters, definition 1 can go right out the window. The one thing Pagans share, in my experience, is that we don't believe in "perfect, omnipotent, or omniscient," at least not as a practical day-to-day definition of godhood. If there is a single originator of the Universe, They have better things to do with Their time than worry about if we're having sex with the wrong sort of people. As for anyone "ruling" the Universe—well, again relying on my own experience, you don't hear about that much either in Pagan thought.

Now, a thought about the phrase "my own experience" before we go any further. My colleague Galina Krasskova, in her brilliant book *Exploring the Northern Tradition: A Guide to the Gods, Lore, Rites, and Celebrations from the Norse, German, and Anglo-Saxon Traditions*, uses a great concept that I am hereby borrowing with credit: the UPG, or Unverified Personal Gnosis. A UPG—the term was apparently first coined in Kat MacMorgan's *Wicca 333* and is commonly used through a lot of the Reconstructuralist community—is a revealed truth about a deity or practice that is received through personal religious work. The example Krasskova uses is that the goddess Freya likes strawberries to be dedicated or sacrificed to her in ritual. Nowhere in the extant body of Norse lore was this ever written down, but enough Ásatrú have discovered it on their own that it's passed into general practice.

Simple enough. Here's the rest of the equation: a lot of what I'm going to cover in this book is UPG, either my own or someone else's. This book is *not* meant to be taken as an authoritative, historical record of pre-Christian practices. There will be prayers and workings in this book; I did not translate them from Middle Norse, Ancient Etruscan, or High Atlantean. There will be spells in this book; I did not receive them from my grandmother in the kitchen. This is information—call it Wisdom if you like—that I have gathered over eighteen years as a Pagan, fifteen years as a Wiccan priest, eight years in Pagan Pride, and three years as an initiated man of the ManKind Project. If I find anyone misquoting this book as gospel truth passed down through the centuries, I will tie them down and make them read the collected works of Bob Larson and Michael Warnke.[2]

Now, back to our definition above.

We can eliminate definitions 3 through 6 almost as easily. We are not talking about idolatry; we are not talking about Brad Pitt; we are not talking about rulers with delusions of godhood; and we are definitely not talking about God in the classic graffiti sense of "Clapton Is God" (though interestingly enough, I can envision a universe where Eric Clapton is the direct manifestation of the Divine—but only while playing guitar). We're starting to run out of options here, but we have one more possibility.

Let's try definition 2 on for size. Wow! We have a working definition. "Believed in and worshiped by a people." Check. "A male deity thought to control some part of nature or reality." Check. "Supernatural powers or attributes." Well, I could quibble about this; in my opinion, the gods are extremely *natural*, and sometimes it's man who's outside of that loop, but other than that semantic point, I can live with it.

So, after we strip away the definitions we don't need, we get it boiled down to this:

"God. (*n.*) A male being of extra-human powers or attributes, believed in or worshiped by a people or peoples, usu-

---

2. Larson and Warnke are two of the more extreme manifestations of Christian evangelical "occult experts." Warnke was a Christian comedian who would lecture on his days as a Satanic witch high priest—all of which turned out to be fiction. Larson is a so-called "occult expert" who lectures police departments. Both of them are the kind of self-appointed truth-distorting "experts" that keep Kerr Cuhulain busy.

ally governing or personifying some element of nature or reality."

That works pretty well, but we still have an interesting sticking point. The book is called *Sacred Paths for Modern Men*, not *Sacred Gods*. Why is that, do you think? Okay, okay, I admit it, it's not a rhetorical question. This book isn't just about the gods, it's about how the gods relate to the men who worship them, follow them, serve them, work with them, love them. This isn't about Them, it's about us—and what Their resurgence, presence, and love mean to us in the modern day.

As men, we are just starting to realize that we, too, have been victimized by the patriarchy, by the power-over structure that has developed in our world over many years. We are starting to learn that the chains we put on women weighed us down as well, and we didn't even see the damned things until they were pulling us under. We have forgotten how to cry, to scream, to hunt, to love, to honor, to teach, to initiate. It is this lack of a spiritual and ancestral heritage that has led many men to the Pagan paths, and it is this heritage we are rebuilding and reclaiming every day.

We rebuild this heritage in a lot of different ways. Some of those ways are constructive. We get back to our primal selves, what Robert Bly called the Wild Man, through work with other men in safe spaces. We express our pain at the roles that society has tried to force us into, through therapy or group work or personal journeying. We rediscover the functional Divine Male through religious, shamanic, or magickal work.

Then there are the destructive ways. Drinking or drugging to excess; emotional, physical, or sexual abuse; escape into the stale clichés of male life expressed through cheap beer commercials, reruns of *Jackass, Girls Gone Wild*, substance abuse, or bad fraternity parties—all these have one thing in common: *Through our destructive habits we hide from the pain we feel at having no sacred male heritage, pain we cannot express because our ability to feel has been systematically crippled by society and by ourselves.* Our tribes are gone, our hunts futile, our emotional defenses laughable. We have nothing. We're just drones.

But it doesn't have to be that way. We can embrace ourselves and demand our sacred nature back. Society took our gods, our tribes, our elders—we can take them back, or make new ones. If this isn't magick I don't know what is; I think rebuilding an entire spiritual archetype, the Sacred Male, is Great Work enough for any lifetime! What this book is about, in the final analysis, is this process. By examining the stories, symbols, reality, and nature of the gods, we examine ourselves, and in Their reality we find the keys to change our own deep male realities for the better.

So this is about *Sacred Paths for Modern Men*—our own, our sons', our fathers', our ancestors', our gods'. This is about rebuilding the tribe that is Pagan Manhood and stepping up to take our rightful place—whether that place be Sacred Consort, Horned Lord, Wise Sage, Trickster, or any of many other names.

Speaking of those Names . . .

II

TWELVE SACRED NAMES

See, in the last few years, we've stumbled.
. . . And when you stumble a lot, you . . .
you start looking at your feet. Well, we have to make
people . . . lift their eyes back to the horizon, and see
the line of ancestors behind us, saying, "Make my life
have meaning." And to our inheritors before us, saying,
"Create the world we will live in."
I mean, we're not just . . . holding jobs and having
dinner. We are in the process of building the future.

—Captain John Sheridan, *Babylon 5*

Humans like symbols, classifications, and systems. In the words of Delenn from *Babylon 5*, "Humans build communities"—not just communities of people but communities of ideas.[3] We learn early in life to identify things by classes: that's food; that's the dog; the dog is not food; don't bite the dog.

As such, while perhaps it would be more comprehensive and fair to examine each male deity as an individual in the history of pre-Abrahamic faiths, it would also make for a very, very long book that I could never get published. As such, I have identified twelve divine archetypes that I want to examine in greater detail. Note this: not all gods are going to fit here, and some of them are going to fit in more than one classification. (In fact, in my humble assessment, Loki shows up in *at least* five.) In this, we see that gods, like humans, are individuals, and are not easily reduced to single concepts. That's okay! If the gods were just symbols and nothing else, if there were no divine revelations or experience to be

3. Yes, that's two *Babylon 5* quotes in a row. I think *Babylon 5* is one of the greatest stories in history—never mind the fact that it's the best sci-fi television show ever—and I think what creator J. Michael Straczynski had to say about life, spirituality, struggle, nobility, power, good, evil, and destiny is truly, truly incredible.

had, if the gods were *easy*, then we could do this all in our heads while reading Jung instead of casting circles or beating drums around fires.

An important note—and here's where I expect people to unshoulder their flamethrowers—I reserve the right to use "fictional" gods in this work within reason. In my own personal practice, I have gotten more out of Malory's *Le Morte d'Arthur* and Tolkien's *Silmarillion* than I have a lot of the Pagan books of the week. In at least one assessment of the origin of Wicca, the "traditional" pairing of Cernunnos and Aradia actually came ten years after *The Hobbit*. I was never much of a believer in "mytho-seniority" anyway. Early in my Pagan career I got into a very large online battle about a full-moon ritual we did in which we invoked Bombadil and Galadriel. I guess I just still haven't learned, more than fourteen years later.

With that said, here are the Twelve Sacred Names that we will experience together, in no particular order:

I. **The Child**—The Divine Youth who originates all things.

II. **The Lover**—The god who desires, loves, and reaches out.

III. **The Warrior**—The god who draws boundaries and uses force.

IV. **The Trickster**—The joker whose jests may hide lessons.

V. **The Green Man**—The primal spirit of nature.

VI. **The Guide**—The mentor who teaches the quester.

VII. **The Craftsman**—The god who creates with his hands.

VIII. The Destroyer/Challenger—The god who ends—ends things, ends people, ends processes.

IX. The Magician—The transformer and guardian of esoteric knowledge.

X. The King/Elder—The wise and regal god who brings order.

XI. The Healer—The god who closes wounds and brings peace.

XII. The Sacrificed One—The god whose death brings a great change.

Astute readers will notice a similarity here between my work and the work of Robert Moore and Douglas Gillette in their groundbreaking, amazing, I-am-not-worthy *King, Warrior, Magician, Lover*—and indeed, four of our twelve Names come directly from that book. In my judgment—and this is only my judgment—Moore and Gillette's archetypal system is wonderful, but not quite complete enough for a survey of Pagan practice. Nevertheless, I owe them a huge debt.

That said, these Names aren't perfect, nor are they supposed to be the be-all and end-all of divine manhood. Our goal on this journey is to get a feel for each of these archetypes—to experience them through meditation, prayer, and spellwork; to learn a little bit about the gods who are part of these Names; and to pave the way for further exploration in personal practice and study. You will not know everything you need to know about the Trickster when you're done reading this book. (Indeed, one wonders if anyone knows everything they *need* to know about the Trickster; that's part of the fun, isn't it?) Instead, I hope that here we plant a seed that grows through your own personal work and continued religious practice.

In addition, I want to add to the body of poetic ritual that is aimed at the man who is also a Pagan. I will never forget being told once about a man who was really interested in Paganism whose first book was *The Spiral Dance*.[4] He felt really empowered, in touch, together—until he was asked to breathe from his uterus. That's not to say that *The Spiral Dance* isn't brilliant—far from it. I'm on my third copy and working on my fourth; they get worn out through use.

But what Starhawk did in *The Spiral Dance* is create spiritual poetry for the Pagan female soul. And with a few exceptions (the work of Galen Gillotte and Ceisiwr Serith comes to mind) there's very little of that for gods, for men. Spirituality for me is mystic, poetic, and experiential, and that's what I want to share with you.

---

4. Starhawk, *The Spiral Dance* (San Francisco: HarperSanFrancisco, 1999). Starhawk's work is one of the three or four most important Pagan books out there. Starhawk is responsible for tying Eclectic Wicca to political activism and feminism, and this work remains a groundbreaking reference on Paganism, feminist thought, and Pagan social justice. If there is a complaint to be made about *Spiral Dance*, it's that to some people it comes off as terribly gynocentric. Starhawk's later work and social activism has also been of an extremely left-wing bent.

III

THE DIVINE CHILD
APRON STRINGS AND WISER THINGS

A child of five would understand this.
Send someone to fetch a child of five.

—Groucho Marx

There may be no more potent symbol in Western thought than that of the Divine Child. After all, once you strip the tinsel and Santa Claus away from our most celebrated and financially lucrative holiday, at its core Christmas is one big birthday party for a child who never grows up. A good deal of our literature—references that run the gamut from Peter Pan to Harry Potter to *Shane*—tells the eternal story of the boy who becomes a man, or the boy who won't become a man no matter how much it may be the right or natural thing to do.

Why does this symbol grip us so? I think it's because the power it represents is so incredibly primal and vital to mature manhood—and yet conversely it is one of the easiest to twist into a dark reflection of itself. How many of us know an adult male who is shading his way towards forty—or even older—but is still trying to be the frat guy with the sports car whose primary drive is toward scoring and getting drunk weekend after weekend? Youth has become our Holy Grail, and we're willing to ride a whole bunch of destriers into the ground to get to it.

Yet the Divine Child *in its proper place and time* is incredibly powerful. In the words of Robert Moore and Douglas

Gillette, " . . . the Divine Child is the archetypical energy that prefigures the mature masculine energy of the King."[5] Or, to put it in simpler terms, the Divine Child is by its nature a gateway to the adult archetypes that form a functional man —or, if you prefer, a functional God.

One of the major steps in the development of the Divine Child is that of separating him from his Mother. The eternal dichotomy of being a young boy—whether one is mortal or divine—is that we start out as being part of Mother, and at some point we must draw the line and become our own person, become our own man. A number of societal maladjustments among modern men—the objectification of women, various forms of self-abuse, and the unhealthy identification with a group of other males—comes from the conflict with the mother-figure that looms so large in our psyches. We talk about cutting the apron strings, yet even that metaphor is laced with violence. (Me, I prefer the idea that the apron strings fall away on their own. On the other hand, I didn't cut mine until I was twenty-one, and it was quite the blow-up. My mother didn't speak to me for eight months.)

As male Pagans, we try very hard to rise above that trap. Yet we often find ourselves in places within our own subculture where we get stuck in roles of pointless rebellion and posturing. I have seen my share of witch-wars and antago-

---

5. Robert Moore and Douglas Gillette, *King, Warrior, Magician, Lover: Rediscovering the Archetypes of the Mature Masculine* (San Francisco: HarperSanFrancisco, 1991), 19.

nists[6] within the Pagan community, and I would say from a rough, nonscientific recollection that 80 percent of them have been male. What is an antagonist—or anyone undermining community—but an armchair tyrant, an angry child, crying out for attention?

Yet the Divine Child is powerful in his own right. He is the first archetype of drawing boundaries, of establishing the self that serves as the foundation for the great magickal advice "know thyself." He is the spirit of beginnings, of the first steps, the Fool of the major arcana, the spirit of Yule. And finally he is the Young Hero, the avenging Son who steps forward into his power.

The Tale of Eros

The element of setting boundaries, of drawing a line between Youth and Mother, is illustrated powerfully in the story of Psyche and Eros:

> *Psyche, a mortal princess, had gained the reputation for being as beautiful as Aphrodite, the Greek goddess of beauty. Aphrodite, naturally, became jealous and angry, and she sent her son Eros, the Greek god of romantic love and a Divine Child, to shoot Psyche with his arrows so that she would fall in love with a hideous monster. Eros*

---

6. As Kenneth Haugk put it: "Antagonist—individuals who, on the basis of non-substantiative evidence, go out of their way to make insatiable demands, usually attacking the person or performance of others. These attacks are selfish in nature, tearing down rather than building up, and are frequently directed at those in a leadership capacity." The quote is from Kenneth Haugk's brilliant *Antagonists in the Church* (Minneapolis: Augsburg Fortress, 1988), 21.

was also known as Cupid, in case that arrows-of-love thing sounds familiar.

Meanwhile, Psyche's father was told by the Oracle at Delphi that Psyche would not marry a mortal man, but rather would marry something that flew through the night and whose power was so great that not even Father Zeus could withstand it. He was told to take her to the top of a mountain and leave her, and she would be transported to her intended.

Needless to say, her intended was Eros, who upon seeing her beauty found himself quite incapable of carrying out his mother's wishes. Instead of punishing her, he kept Psyche for himself—yet forbade her to ever see his face. His palace was rich, and Psyche had anything she wanted, though in time she began to wonder who this was she was married to. When her sisters came to the palace to visit and badgered her about who her husband was, she broke Eros's commandment and looked in on him while he was sleeping. Her oil lamp spilled on his shoulder, and he awoke. Saying "there is no love without trust," Eros left Psyche.[7]

Now, Psyche did eventually get Eros back after performing a number of ridiculously difficult labors for Aphrodite. (One assumes that Aphrodite was pretty peeved about the whole thing to begin with, and took a great deal of mother-in-law-like frustration out on Psyche.) In the end, Zeus made

---

7. All tales are my retelling and my responsibility, unless sources are otherwise cited.

Psyche immortal, and she joined Eros on Olympus. (Nice deal for Psyche, huh?)

I find it interesting that Eros took Psyche back. After all, she'd proven herself untrustworthy, hadn't she? Why go back to that? I think the answer lies in the Divine Child's ability to forgive and believe the best about everyone. The gift of the Child is to see the divine in all things, even someone utterly lost; I am reminded of the scene in Steven Spielberg's *Hook* (which, incidentally, I like a whole bunch, despite what most critics had to say) when one of the Lost Boys suddenly stops and takes Robin Williams' face in his hands, turns it one way or another, and suddenly says in wonder, "Oh, *there* you are, Peter."[8] The Divine Child can see the goodness of childhood in others.

The Divine Child is also utterly and completely under assault in our society. I'm going to sound like a fundamentalist Christian here for a moment, so brace yourself—children in our society, *especially boys*, are at terribly frightening risk because they are exposed too early to violence. Video games, cartoons, schoolhouse violence—all these serve to destroy the Divine Child within by making a boy constantly afraid and looking for attack from outside.

I have seen far too many parents blithely ignore rating systems and content, and their children pay for it. I once asked a covener about her son's behavior, which was difficult in the extreme; I found out that she was letting her eight-year-old boy play *Grand Theft Auto III*. I found that irresponsible and reprehensible. How can you be a Wiccan, a religion

---

8. *Hook*, DVD, directed by Steven Spielberg (1991; Culver City, CA: Sony Pictures Home Entertainment)..

that honors the cycle of life, and not take into account the natural cycle of child to adult? In order for the Divine Child to fully manifest in the adult, he must be kept safe until it is time for him to move *naturally* into greater awareness of the reality of the world.

Eros is the dichotomy, the Divine Child in his full power—able to forgive and yet still drawing boundaries and separating from Mother powerfully and decisively. He refused Aphrodite's will because his heart said to do otherwise. Then, when Psyche broke their agreement, he walked away from her as well. In this, we see the Divine Child's power to take the first steps towards mature masculinity.

The Tale of Lugh

Another manifestation of the Divine Child can be seen in the Fool, the card of the major arcana symbolizing stepping forth onto a new road and a new life—often involving a new name or a new identity. In Welsh mythology, Lugh gained his name as a child through the guidance of Gwydion and through his own cleverness. This pairing of the young apprentice and the old master is a symbolic transfer of wisdom and power that is a constant thread throughout classical and new myth—young heroes come with mentors and masters, from Zeus to Albus Dumbledore.

So it was with Lugh:

> Lugh was found by Gwydion in a chest, and raised by a wet nurse, and then brought to court. He was reared by Gwydion, who grew to love him—and one day accompanied him to the castle of Arianrhod, who was his mother.

Arianrhod did not wish to acknowledge Lugh, and as such cursed him that he would not receive a name from anyone until she had named him. (He had no name at this time, and you can be sure Arianrhod didn't intend to change that.) Through Gwydion's counsel and a good bit of subterfuge, Lugh tricked Arianrhod into naming him, amazing her with a shot he made to slay a wren. She then swore that he would have no arms or armor unless he received them from her hand.

With Gwydion's counsel again, Lugh received arms from Arianrhod by making her believe that her castle was under siege while he and Gwydion were there, in disguise as bards. By this time Arianrhod was in a bit of a pique, so she swore he would never have a wife of a race that inhabited the earth. In response to this, Gwydion and Math, a great wizard and leader, fashioned Lugh a wife out of flowers, Bloudewedd, and they were married.

While it would be easy to generalize this story as another rebellion against a mother-figure (one suspects that having either Aphrodite or Arianrhod as a mother would be tough), in my judgment it's a little more complex than that. Lugh has the advantage of a mentor, a wise elder, and follows his advice to come up with a solution to his challenges that meets them rather than ignores them.

Lugh manifests the next step in the Divine Child's development. Having successfully separated himself from the identification with the Mother, he must then learn his own way to approach the realities and riddles of the world. Through the mentor or the Guide (again, an archetype that we'll explore in greater detail later), he begins to develop his own independent reality, his own approaches, his own solutions—dare I say his own style?

That elder energy is lacking in our modern society, and it shows. Our young men don't have elders, and as such they either don't learn from those who have gone before them or they learn the wrong lessons from their peers. As Pagans, we are more cognizant of the roles of elders than most, and even we are lacking. Formal mentoring and eldering relationships are still rare in Paganism, just as they are rare in our society. That energy has been systematically devalued by a desire to see people as interchangeable parts in a greater structure. To mentor a man or a boy, you have to see him as a unique individual who cannot be reduced to a stereotype, who cannot be classified and cubbyholed. That kind of one-on-one interaction is almost a lost art—but it is a lost art we are reclaiming.

From my own experience, it took a wise elder who bothered to take the time with me to turn me into a functional man. That happened when I was in my early thirties; it should have happened much earlier. (We'll discuss the Elder in much greater detail later.)

The Tale of Horus

The final face of the Divine Child to consider is that of the avenger of a fallen or lost father. While this has become grist for the mill of a great number of B-movies, the original concept of the Son-Avenger is a potent and a very old symbol—no place better expressed, perhaps, than in the myth of Horus, Isis, and Osiris.

> Osiris was the great ruler of Egypt, having brought civilization—writing, law, science, the arts—to that magnificent land through his own efforts and the inventions of Thoth. After raising up the Egyptians, Osiris next traveled forth to bring his guidance to other peoples, leaving Isis, his bride, as his regent.
>
> But all this progress had a price. Apep, the serpent spirit of darkness, was angered by the efforts of Osiris and killed him. Isis and her infant son, Horus, fled into the marshland of the Nile Delta, and Apep's darkness ruled over all. When he was old enough, however, Horus, the child of the Sun, came forth, defeated Apep, and avenged his father.
>
> During various periods of Egyptian history, the villain changed—Set became the black-hearted killer after the overthrow of the Hyksos, the foreign conquerors who had adopted Set as their patron deity—and various details were added. In one version of the tale, Horus was actually the resurrected Osiris, come again to continue his guidance and wisdom. But the son—the Divine Child avenging a fallen father—remained.

The story of Horus is the eternal tale of generations changing hands, of the sons becoming the fathers. If, as Moore and Gillette say, the Divine Child "prefigures" the energy of the King, then Horus is a perfect manifestation of that prefiguration and a powerful source of energy in times of change and trial.

Again, this is the cycle of growth. The Divine Child has moved past the Mother, received the mentor's wisdom, and is now fully functional and actualized, capable of taking his own action as he sees fit. In short, he's grown up, and decided what he wants to be. Horus shows that final step—and I find it interesting that some versions of the Horus story say Horus is either the return of Osiris or a manifestation of Ra. The Child becomes the Father, and the cycle continues.

In life, it's common that we, in effect, become our fathers. In working with men in the ManKind Project, I've found that many men's personal issues come from trying to emulate the example their fathers gave them—or, worse, repeating the same patterns their fathers exemplified. This can manifest as anything from working too hard or too long (because that's what Dad did) to the self-perpetuating cycle of physical, emotional, or sexual abuse. Our wounds as men often stem from our fathers. Horus can serve as a source of guidance for men who are in this trap, stuck in these patterns; his bright solar energy and pure power can be evoked to supply strength to break out of a pattern of reputation. Conversely, Horus can serve as a symbol for a father or father-figure we as men would like to model ourselves after.

Even when the Child becomes an adult, there's an important undercurrent to consider. One of the important pieces we try to remember in the ManKind Project is that many of our personal reactions, opinions, and default emotions are formed at a very early age. I know in my own work that when I went underneath my base reactions to people and occurrences, I often found that I was responding based on programming I had received when I was very young, as young as two or three years old. It's extremely difficult to get to those messages; often we're so far out of touch with our Divine Child, our inner child, that we don't realize we're even hearing the messages. There's a tape running in our head, repeating the message over and over again, and we rarely even realize it's there.

The Child is always with us. Other archetypes may come and go, but we are never completely free of the Child, the lessons he learned as a child, and the desires he has (more on that later).

In summary, the Divine Child is a face of both God and Man, a metaphor and a personification of change, growth, rebirth, and the beginning of the Great Work. He is potency, potential, and power, and the guardian and embodiment of the thresholds we all pass through every day of our lives.

For Further Thought

Are my reactions in my everyday life manifestations of the lessons I learned as a child?

Do I still know how to play and to feel openly?

Have I truly created my own self independent of my upbringing?

MAGICKAL WORKING

Speaking to Your Inner Child

Before we get into the working, there are some basic guidelines I want to set down for all the magickal workings in this book.

1. In an ideal world, we would all have consecrated magickal temples where we keep our tools, do our rituals, and generally behave like magicians and priests. We do not, however, live in an ideal world. It's likely, therefore, that you

will do these rituals in a corner of your bedroom, in your garage, or in your living room after the kids go to bed. That's okay—don't get all stressed about it. The temple is within, not without.

2. Magickal tools are great. They're not, however, necessary. I won't tell you that you have to have anything save an open heart and a searching mind. If you can afford sandalwood incense, silver ewers for water, and carved wooden staves, great. If you're living on ramen noodles and Kraft dinner, take care of yourself first. (And eat some vegetables, for the God's sake.)

3. Trust your feelings, young Jedi. In other words, if your intuition says that it would work better for you to change, add, or omit details of these rituals, do. Nothing is going to jump out and eat your soul, and I won't show up and smite you.

4. Cast circles exist for a *reason*. When you are casting a circle and invoking the direction, you are claiming a piece of the Universe as yours, and declaring it safe space for you to do deep, transformative work in. Keep in mind as you cast your circle and invoke your directions for magickal use that you are setting up protection, safe space, holy space as you see it. This isn't protection from some sort of astral bugaboo, but from the stray energies and random influences that can affect us, especially when we are open to wisdom and energies from Somewhere Else.

With all that said . . .

Recommended Tools

- Paper, pencil, crayons, other drawing supplies as desired
- Some meditative incense—sandalwood, clove, rose, whatever works for you. I like to use my own smudge instead (see appendix I) but it is a bit messier
- A trigger for your childhood memories—more on this later

Calling the Directions

Face each direction as you call it. For the fifth direction, cross your hands over your heart.

East: *I call you, elders and spirits of the East. The colors are the rose of sunrise, yellow of morning, the gray of the mist of dawn. This is the direction of Air, of the Divine Child, the Youth, the Lover, the man beginning his road. Hail and welcome, spirits of the East!*

South: *I call you, elders and spirits of the South. The colors are the red of blood, the orange of fire, the silver of steel. This is the direction of Fire, of the Warrior, the Craftsman, the Challenger, the man at the height of his power. Hail and welcome, spirits of the South!*

West: *I call you, elders and spirits of the West. The colors are the blue of twilight, the black of shadows and mysteries, the slate gray-blue of the sea. This is the direction of Water, of the Magician, the Sacrificed One, the Trickster-shaman, the man with the knowledge and compassion to find out the truth. Hail and welcome, spirits of the West!*

> **North:** *I call you, elders and spirits of the North. The colors are the green and brown of Earth, the gray of stone, the white of frost and snow. This is the direction of Earth, of the Elder, the King, the Guide, the man at the height of his wisdom and elder grace. Hail and welcome, spirits of the North!*
>
> **Soul:** *I call you, elders and spirits of the Spirit and Soul. The colors are the gold of the inner power of men and the purple of the spirit. This is the direction of the Self, the Axis Mundi, the place where all other directions meet. Hail and welcome, spirits of the Spirit and Soul!*

When you have called in the directions, find a comfortable place to sit. Before the ritual has begun, you should find some symbol of your childhood, something tangible that appeals to one or more of your senses—a childhood toy, a recording of a favorite song, a scent or taste, something that to you signifies the young boy you once were.

At this time, turn the lights down—or off if you prefer—and concentrate on the trigger or symbol of your childhood. With your eyes closed, touch, hear, taste, smell this symbol, and remember with all of your might the child you once were. What would that child say if he was here? What wisdom would he have for you?

Take up the pencil or art supplies and begin, without looking, to write, draw, or otherwise inscribe the message and wisdom from your inner child, the little boy you once were. Let the message flow without worrying if it's good enough or drawn well enough. Use your nondominant hand if you like in order to better get in touch with your unconscious self.

When you have finished, return slowly to the place and time in which you began the working and open your eyes. Read the message you wrote, or look at the picture. It may not make sense right away, but keep it with you and refer to it over the next week or so. Let your unconscious mind percolate. Make sure you keep a dream journal by your bed to document anything that might come up as you sleep. Once you have finished documenting the message, take a moment and ground yourself back into the now.

RITUAL OF AFFIRMATION

Coming of Age

For me, one of the most vital breakdowns in our current society is how we handle young men who are coming of age.

A young woman has an obvious biological sign that she has taken her first step towards maturity. A young man—not so much. When you add in the fact that young men are under assault in our culture by violence, sexuality, and other content in media for which they're just not ready, you create a situation where a young man/older boy rarely knows where he is, much less who he is.

This ritual is designed to address that to some extent; to provide a clear marker where a young man's status, both internally and externally, changes.

This ritual was originally published in *PanGaia* magazine in a different form, and is reproduced with thanks and love.

In addition to the young man, generally between the ages of twelve and sixteen, who is coming of age, this ceremony should include a circle of men, including, if possible, one man of around twenty (the Youth), one around thirty-five (the Warrior), one around fifty (the King), and one around seventy (the Elder). A simple altar should be laid with a God and Goddess candle, quarter candles, and symbols of the elements: a wand, a blade, a cup, and a stone. The room should begin as dark as possible; if the ritual participants can memorize the dialogue so that they can begin in complete darkness, so much the better. Before the ritual, a small bag of some sort, suitable for ritual use—cloth, leather, whatever seems appropriate—should be obtained for the young man.

The Youth brings the young man into the ritual space. He should enter in simple ritual clothing; no ritual tools, jewelry, and so forth. The Warrior meets him at the edge of the space:

Warrior: You have come to begin your quest on the path to manhood. Are you willing to begin to take on those responsibilities, to act with virtue and honor, to begin to be self-reliant, to be your own hero?

Young man affirms in his own words.

Youth: You have taken the first step on the road to manhood. Manhood is a hard thing to describe. Our society would have you believe it involves power over things: possessions, women, excess. We here, though, know that manhood is sacred.

Warrior: Manhood is about being a warrior, about fighting for what you know to be right.

King: Manhood is about being noble, keeping your word, honoring others.

Elder: Manhood is about being wise, and learning that wisdom comes through pain and experience.

The young man is brought to the center of the circle, before the altar.

Youth: I call to the East, the spirits of Air! At the beginning of the day, we honor the beginning of the road, the morning from which life springs. Hail and welcome, spirits of the East, essence of Air!

Warrior: I call to the South, the spirits of Fire! At the noontide of the day, we honor the heart of the road, the bright moment in which we are strongest, fastest, fleetest, best. Hail and welcome, spirits of the South, essence of Fire!

King: I call to the West, the spirits of Water! At the end of the day, we honor the winding down of the road, the twilight in which we first begin to experience the unknown. Hail and welcome, spirits of the West, essence of Water!

Elder: I call to the North, the spirits of Earth! In the heart of the night, we honor the end of the road, the dark midnight in which we finish our quest and begin the spiral anew. Hail and welcome, spirits of the North, essence of Earth!

Youth: We welcome the Great Goddess, Maiden, Mother, Crone—She who is the shadow to our light, the light to our shadow. Without the one, there cannot be the other. Hail, Great Goddess!

Elder: We welcome the Great God, king, warrior, magician, lover—He who is the center of our manhood, the root from which we spring. Without the one, there cannot be the other. Hail, Great God!

The four men move to surround the young man.

Youth: As you begin your quest, I lay this charge on you. Honor women. They are not objects; they are not prizes to be fought over; they have their own mysteries, and you must honor them. Treat women with respect. Treat them with dignity. Treat them as you treat yourself, with honor. Do you so swear?

(*affirmation*)

Warrior: As you begin your quest, I lay this charge on you. Honor the earth. It is the Mother from which all life springs; it is sacred and the reflection of the sacred, the cauldron of Cerridwen from which all life springs. Treat it as you treat yourself, with care. Do you so swear?

(*affirmation*)

King: As you begin your quest, I lay this charge on you. Honor other men. Each human being is on their own quest; act with kindness and care towards all. Respect them, support them, love them. Value your friends and brothers as you value yourself. Do you so swear?

(*affirmation*)

Elder: As you begin your quest, I lay this charge on you. Honor the mystery. You are divine; I am divine; all things are interconnected. Honor the diversity within that. Have faith, believe, accept love and miracles for what they are. Do you so swear?

(*affirmation*)

Elder: Then what do you choose to be your quest for this time in your life, and do you take a name in circle to reflect that quest?

Here, the young man can read a statement, make an oath, whatever. It should be prepared beforehand; it should reflect something deep and valid to the young man that he wants to make his Great Work for now.

All Men: So witnessed.

King: Then, [*name*], we so witness your oaths and your purpose, and we welcome you to the society of men, the long road of the quest of all who have gone before you.

Elder: As an Elder of our tribe, I commend to you the watchword of the Divine Child: *potential.* May you remember it as you continue on your life journey. May you spend every moment attempting to live up to the potential the God has given you in this incarnation.

Warrior: I present you with this talisman of your coming of age (*presents the young man with a bag containing one sacred object—stone, shell, rune, whatever—from each man in the ritual*). Many cultures throughout history have presented young men with magick bags with which to do their personal magickal and shamanic work. May this, our gift, serve you well.

Youth: (*lays hand on the young man's forehead*) I bless you in the name of the Divine Child.

King: (*to the directions as he speaks*) The Earth of determination, the Water of love, the Fire of the spirit, and the Air of wisdom; we thank and bless their spirits, knowing they are with us always. May they guide you on your quest.

Youth: We thank the Great Goddess, She who is our other soul, for standing with us tonight.

Elder: We thank the Great God, He who is our root and our spirit, for standing with us tonight.

Warrior: Go now, and begin your journey. We are with you always. Come to us should you need our wisdom. We are your brothers.

The young man should be instructed to keep the talisman as the beginning of his collection of sacred objects.

IV

THE LOVER

CONQUEST, UNION, AND SURRENDER

The lover knows much more about absolute good and universal beauty than any logician or theologian, unless the latter, too, be lovers in disguise.

—George Santayana

A beer commercial sings the praises of a "wing man," a friend who goes out with a man and keeps the ugly or annoying woman company while the man moves in on the cute girl for sexual conquest.

A group of adult males gather around the water cooler, bragging quietly about cheating on their wives while adding in the occasional homophobic comment.

A college student slips Rohypnol into his date's drink.

Is it any wonder that the Lover is one of the archetypes that your average Western male is the furthest from? Our relationship with the Lover, with rare exceptions, has devolved into adolescent sniggering and cheap laughs. We dishonor our partners and we dishonor ourselves with our behavior.

How did we get into this mess? We could point fingers at everything from organized religion to television to the proliferation of drugs that treat erectile dysfunction. (You don't believe me? A divorce was granted in the United Kingdom on the grounds that Viagra made the husband too sexually demanding.[9]) When it comes down to it, though, it's counterproductive to look for something to blame. Blame won't

---

9. Judith Duffy, "First UK Viagra divorce," *Daily Record* (Glasgow), April 19, 2004.

fix the problem. How we got into this mess isn't the issue; more importantly, how do we get out of it?

Most men want to be happy. Most men don't want to be alone. Yet we often behave in a way that means we will be just that. The common thread in this behavior seems to be a lack of honor and accountability. We think we can cut corners, play false with our partners, play games with other people—in short, we think that life can be like a beer commercial. And too often, the crash men have when they realize that's *not* the case can be life-shattering.

The Lover seeks union and intimacy—not necessarily sexual union, though that can indeed be a part of it—in an accountable and honorable framework. The Lover is also the part of the man that seeks the ecstatic, the transcendent, and the emotional. And finally, in a dichotomy that comes from our essential human nature, the Lover is also the sensualist, the hedonist, and the connoisseur of the finer things in life. When all these things come together, we achieve ecstasy— but it's a conjunction of supreme rarity.

The reality of the situation, usually sad, is reflected in the media. How many happy couples are there on television? As Pagans we believe in magick and that the symbol creates the reality; how much energy does our modern media give to the thought-pattern that the Lover cannot exist? Compare the number of happy, ordinary couples to the number of miserable or somehow star-crossed ones. Now add in that the media shows us many more celebrity divorces than happy celebrity relationships, and what sort of magickal message are we getting about the Lover and his energy?

In one interpretation, the Wiccan Rede says, "An thou harm none, do as thou wilt." This is the essential distillation of the creed of the Lover, and too often we as men indulge ourselves in the second part while conveniently forgetting the first. Eventually, the truth will come to light, one way or another, and we will find ourselves destroying the intimacy we have worked so hard to build. The only answer is to remain transparent and honest, to be willing to do whatever it takes to achieve the ecstasy and the intimacy we desire.

The Tale of the Divine Consort

The Great Goddess is eternal. She may wear different faces at different times of the year, but She is always present.

Her Consort, however, is finite—yet he is also eternal. He is born at Yule, the Winter Child whose birth heralds the return of the Sun. On Imbolc, Brigidmas, he is the Young Mage who evokes the fires that warm a February night. At Ostara he meets his Lady, and at Beltaine they are married. Litha, Midsummer, is where he is at his height of power—but he is also told by the Faerie Queen that he must sacrifice himself so that the harvest will come again.

He dies at Lammas, John Barleycorn, his blood going forth to ensure another year's grain. At Mabon, he is mourned as he travels across the Sea to the Land of the Dead. And at Samhain, he returns, breaking free of the darkness and throwing open the gates so that our honored dead can return to us as well, for one night. He is finite. He dies. He shares that death with us, the reflection of our human nature. Yet like our souls that return again and again on the wheel of rebirth, he too returns—and his

return each year means that we can, for a night, on Sam-
hain, rest in the company of our honored ancestors again.

There may be nowhere that modern Wiccan men see this energy as well as that of the Divine Consort. The Divine Consort is a Green God, the spirit of the returning light and fertility of spring and summer. His death is the harvest; his return, the return of the sun; and his marriage to the eternal Goddess at Beltane, the source of divine and human sensuality and sexuality. The Consort is a ubiquitous symbol of male and female union, of sexual love.

However, there's another, deeper side to this concept. The Divine Consort is, in many ways, a foreordained sacrifice, who subsumes his desires and his needs to the necessity of the cycle of the seasons. In my own tradition, Storyteller Wicca, he receives the knowledge of his own death at Midsummer and freely accepts the burden of death and rebirth so that the seasons will continue to turn and the balance of life will remain stable and self-renewing. This is a brilliant reflection of the accountable and honorable side of the Lover. While I'm not a big fan of the concept of martyrdom per se, the Divine Consort sees what must be done and does it for the sake of the love he holds.

Sometimes, there is a greater cause that requires us to give up our love in the short term. From Achilles and Patroclus to the cops and firefighters who went up the towers one more time on 9/11, the concept of true sacrifice and heroism is a thread that is always with us.

It's also something we're constantly barraged with in the media—a romantic archetype that is presented as the ultimate in male excellence. To which I say: nonsense. There are times and places when a sacrifice is necessary, but the romanticization of the concept has resulted in false expectations for all men. Sure, Randy Quaid looks good when he flies into the alien ship in *Independence Day*—but his kids are still orphans and he's still dead. We have to remain accountable to the truth in the concept of the sacrifice of the Lover. The truth does hurt sometimes.

Partly that's because the Lover listens well to the unspoken word, understands the unseen reality. The Lover is capable of a sort of intuitive divination, understanding what must be done and what should be done without any form of rational input. When a man brings home roses without knowing why and later finds out his partner has just had a terrible day—that is the Lover's intuition speaking to him.

In the long run, though, the Lover is a mixture of impulses: sacrifice, hedonism, intuition, and ecstasy. It's a delicate balance and one that easily becomes disrupted; this accountability in love is the essence of heroism, a concept men throughout the ages have held dear. Self-sacrifice for love and for a greater ideal is a potent, potent symbol—and one that many men have lost touch with in the era of "me first" and "greed is good."

The Tale of Krishna

Of course, love doesn't always have to be that basic or that simple. In the tales of Krishna from Hindu belief, we see love as the transcendent and eternal ideal of the Divine's reason for existence. In the *Bhagavad Gita*, Krishna reveals himself as God and speaks to various truths about himself and his relationship to humanity. One of those truths—perhaps the central truth—is that Krishna *is* love, and all things have a relationship to him in love.

> *Krishna was foreordained to kill the demon-king Kamsa, and as such was taken from his family and hidden with a family of cowherders. There he grew up. His greatest friend and soul mate was the cowherdess Radha; even though she married and Krishna eventually went off to have adventures and bring justice to many people, Radha remained faithful to Krishna in her heart. Her love for Krishna was so pure, so steadfast, that she too became a goddess in time, Krishna's consort, and in that pure love Krishna surrenders himself to her, the eternal union of worshiped and worshiper, divine and human, god and goddess. Krishna becomes the spirit of divine love, of ecstatic union, in part because of Radha's love for him.*

Wow. That's some powerful stuff.

In simpler terms, Krishna becomes love because he is shown love. As men, often we have lacked love in our lives, lacked emotional expression or intimacy. We get told to hide our feelings, suck it up, stop crying—and we wall ourselves off from the world, cutting ourselves off from the Divine within and without.

Very few of us are lucky enough to have our Radha. Yet we can become the Lover within by the simple expediency of expressing our emotions in a straightforward and honest way. We can stop lying to ourselves and others. We can admit when we hurt, when we cry, when we are wounded, and we can as men ask our gods to help us feel and deal with those feelings. Only then can we, as Krishna, seek the great joy that comes with limitless love.

The other option is to put limits on ourselves, and to give in to the shadow of the Lover. If the Lover refuses to honor other men's boundaries, we end up with a mythological shadow of gargantuan proportions—the Love-Stealer.

He goes by many names—Lancelot, Mars, Paris. He is the third side of the triangle, the interloper that ruins harmony between lovers, and the tragic flaw that undoes many a hero (including himself). The Love-Stealer brought down both Camelot and Troy, and he can probably claim credit for the destruction of a few hundred covens as well.

It's easy to look at the Love-Stealer and say that he's a man who has decided to step beyond the limits of an existing relationship. I disagree. Rather, I see him as a figure whose selfishness is a self-imposed limit. He's bought into the myth that there's only one love for him, and he has decided to hold another man's vows, intentions, and goals in little to no respect.

What's boggling to me is that there are more examples of the Love-Stealer in mythology than there are dedicated lovers. The concept of conquest, theft, and ownership of love seems to be endemic to the male consciousness—and frankly I think it's an archetype that as men we are well quit of. I'm not talking about consensual polyamory; that's an entirely different situation, and it'll be something I address later. I'm talking about dishonesty and a lack of accountability in matters of the heart. As in many other facets of our lives as men, this lack of accountability will come back to haunt us unless we keep the Lover's true intentions fully in mind.

For Further Thought

Am I in integrity with my partner and myself right now? If I don't have a partner, am I behaving with integrity in order to have the best chance to achieve my goals in love?

Am I romanticizing my sacrificial streak?

Have I or am I stealing love from someone else?

MAGICKAL WORKING

Seeking a Partner in Love

Ah, love spells. There's little, if anything, that can cause quite as much of a ruckus as a group of Pagans, witches, and magick-workers discussing love spells. Are they ethical? If so, under what circumstances are they ethical? Should you do them?

All I can counsel you to do is to make your own decision, but here's my take on it: *you cannot compel someone else to fall in love with you.* If you do a spell to get Trixie the Goth Waitress to bed you and wed you, then unless you're the greatest magick worker in human history it's very likely that it will do you little good. Buy her black roses instead.

Magick works on shifting the currents of reality. The worker of magick rides the waves like a surfer and learns how to affect those waves so that the desired path becomes the path of least resistance. But the path cannot, at least at our level of magickal knowledge, defy consensual reality. (After 2011, all bets are off.)

This "love" spell, therefore, is designed to bring you what you desire, but for the sake of your own expectations, don't put too specific a name to it, or you'll just be wasting some perfectly good paper, ribbon, and smudge.

With all that said . . .

Recommended Tools

- Two pieces of paper: one red, one gold
- A piece of royal blue ribbon, cord, or yarn
- Some sort of writing instrument you're comfortable with
- Smudge or incense and a white candle

Light your smudge and call the directions (page 262).

Take a moment and just breathe, centering yourself. List in your mind the qualities of your ideal lover. Don't hold back; think big. You are asking the Universe for your heart's desire. This is not a time to cut corners.

When you have that image in your mind, light the white candle, transferring the passion and the energy of the image in your mind to the flame of the candle. Take the red piece of paper and write down seven words that describe your ideal. Then take the gold piece of paper and write down seven words that describe your best qualities as a lover. Think of it as writing a personal ad to the Universe but without the hyperbole. Be honest.

Once those are both completed, roll the gold piece of paper inside the red piece of paper, accepting that the Universe will give you your ideal and have it embrace you. Then tie a loop of the royal blue ribbon—royal blue signifying emotional ideals—around the roll of paper. Say the following:

Of the Lover I ask this boon:
I ask for my heart's desire and my love
Letting it harm no one and for the best for all.

Let my wish and my will and these twice seven words
Be tied together as these papers are tied.

Ground the energy into the embrace of Mother Earth and Father Sky, feeling the connection between the two flow through you, providing you with energy and the love of the gods. When you are content, extinguish the candle.

You may either burn the paper, cast it into running water, or bury it.

RITUAL OF AFFIRMATION

Stepping into Independent Life

At one point in history, men who were stepping forth into their own lives were called journeymen. This was both a literal term (often the second stage of mastery of a craft or profession called upon a man to become an itinerant practitioner of his chosen path) and a metaphorical one—the metaphor being that life is a journey begun when a man leaves the house of his childhood.

This ceremony is designed to honor and solemnize that moment of stepping forth.[10]

This ceremony should include a circle of men, including, if possible, one man of around twenty (the Youth), one around thirty-five (the Warrior), one around fifty (the King), and one around seventy (the Elder). A simple altar should

---

10. This principle applies to a lot of these rituals: *you're ready when you're ready.* A great number of these rituals are written so that a man steps into them when he decides he's ready to step into them. There are guidelines for each one, but fundamentally the candidate has to decide that it's his time.

be laid with a God and Goddess candle, quarter candles, and symbols of the elements: a wand, a blade, a cup, and a stone.

The candidate enters the circle in comfortable clothing, preferably barefoot. He should, if possible, carry into the circle a backpack or satchel containing his personal magickal and spiritual tools.

> **Warrior:** You enter this circle to begin your life as an independent man, stepping into his life role and personal path. You may go away from here, or stay home; you may continue with schooling, or begin a career. No matter what the circumstances, you are no longer a child in your father's house but a man in your own right. Are you prepared to take on this responsibility?
>
> *Candidate states his affirmation in his own words.*
>
> **Youth:** You are now on the road of manhood. Manhood is a hard thing to describe. Our society would have you believe it involves power over things, possessions, women, excess. We here, though, know that manhood is sacred.
>
> **Warrior:** Manhood is about being a warrior, about fighting for what you know to be right.
>
> **King:** Manhood is about being noble, keeping your word, honoring others.
>
> **Elder:** Manhood is about being wise and learning that wisdom comes through pain and experience.
>
> *The candidate is brought to the center of the circle, before the altar.*

Youth: I call to the East, the spirits of Air! At the beginning of the day, we honor the beginning of the road, the morning from which life springs. Hail and welcome, spirits of the East, essence of Air!

Warrior: I call to the South, the spirits of Fire! At the noontide of the day, we honor the heart of the road—the bright moment at which we are strongest, fastest, fleetest, best. Hail and welcome, spirits of the South, essence of Fire!

King: I call to the West, the spirits of Water! At the end of the day, we honor the winding down of the road, the twilight in which we first begin to experience the unknown. Hail and welcome, spirits of the West, essence of Water!

Elder: I call to the North, the spirits of Earth! In the heart of the night, we honor the end of the road, the dark midnight in which we finish our quest and begin the spiral anew. Hail and welcome, spirits of the North, essence of Earth!

Youth: We welcome the Great Goddess, Maiden, Mother, Crone—She who sends us into the world as individuals to walk the Great Road. Without the one, there cannot be the other. Hail, Great Goddess!

Elder: We welcome the Great God, king, warrior, magician, lover—He who is the initiator of desire, the wellspring of our purpose and our gifts. Without the one, there cannot be the other. Hail, Great God!

The four men move to surround the candidate.

Youth: You have stated your desire to begin your own life path, to step forward as man rather than as child. As you begin this quest, I give you this gift. Live brightly in yourself, drink your cup to the dregs, walk with joy, and find your passion. Do you accept this gift from the gods?

Warrior: I give you this gift. Remain true to yourself, know what matters to you, stand by your principles, and be willing to fight honorably and steadfastly for what you believe is right. Do you accept this gift from the gods?

King: I give you this gift. Be strong in yourself. Take care of yourself—body, mind, and soul. Do not abuse yourself and listen for the voices of the gods, spirits, and ancestors. Do you accept this gift from the gods?

Elder: I give you this gift. Accept questioning yourself, reconsider your beliefs, make no assumptions, and admit your mistakes graciously and with honor. Do you accept this gift from the gods?

The candidate affirms each of these gifts.

Elder: Then state your quest and your goal at this time, and if you have a new name to be used in this circle, state it for us.

Candidate responds.

All Men: So witnessed.

King: Then, [*name*], we so witness your oaths and your purpose, and we welcome you to the society of men and the long road of the quest of all who have gone before you.

Elder: As an Elder of our tribe, I commend to you the watchword of the Lover: *accountability*. May you remember it as you continue on your life journey. May your word be your bond and may you never cause harm through negligence or carelessness.

Warrior: I present you with this talisman of your independent manhood. (*He presents the young man with a staff or walking stick, decorated as seems appropriate.*) Take this and let it be your guide on your journey. As you may seek guidance, comfort, and respite from it, so may you seek these things from this circle of men.

Youth: (*lays hand on the young man's forehead*) I bless you in the name of the Lover. Go forth on this road with your mind open. Listen to your heart and your path will be made clear. Be willing to reach out to those around you, and to let them reach out to you as well.

King: (*to the directions as he speaks*) The Earth of determination, the Water of love, the Fire of the spirit, and the Air of wisdom: we thank and bless their spirits, knowing they are with us always. May they guide you on your quest.

Youth: We thank the Great Goddess, She who is our other soul, for standing with us tonight.

Elder: We thank the Great God, He who is our root and our spirit, for standing with us tonight.

Warrior: Go now and begin your journey. We are with you always. Come to us should you need our wisdom. We are your brothers.

V

THE WARRIOR

SOLDIERS, KNIGHTS,
AND COLLATERAL DAMAGE

Great spirits have always encountered opposition from mediocre minds. The mediocre mind is incapable of understanding the man who refuses to bow blindly to conventional prejudices and chooses instead to express his opinions courageously and honestly.

—Albert Einstein

There are two good reasons that I put these two arche-types, the Lover and the Warrior, back to back. They share two very important qualities or sets of qualities that I want to get out in front of us right at the beginning.

The first is that they are probably the two most dys-functional archetypes currently facing your average West-ern male. Take as our example my favorite microcosmic example of Stupid Man Tricks—the beer commercial. If a beer commercial isn't trying to tell us that if we drink a par-ticular variety of fermented hops and malt we'll be sexually invulnerable, then it usually attempts to link its product with some sort of macho physical activity performed in an unsafe, headstrong, or otherwise moronic fashion.

If it's not something the beer drinkers are doing them-selves—naked bungee jumping, jet-assisted snowboarding, or running with the bulls while wearing cement overshoes —it's a visceral experience involving shoulder pads and men pat-ting other men on the butt. Either way, someone's trying to feed our internal Lover or Warrior a line of marketing bull-stuff—something to which they're particularly vulnerable.

The second and perhaps even more notable reason is that the Lover and the Warrior are mirror images of each other. The

Lover crosses boundaries; the Warrior sets them. The Lover is the archetype by which we reach out to others. The Warrior is the archetype that allows us to protect ourselves, our sense of self, and our personal space, beliefs, and practices.

That's a huge and vital function for men. My opinion, for what it's worth, is that while our default setting is that of cooperation in the face of conflict, men have a desperate need for solitude, for solitary guardianship and effort. In any situation where men work together, the possibility of rivalry and jockeying for position and hierarchy is a very real danger. The Warrior is both our blessing and our bane in that it's what allows us to stay separate and individual, secure in our own talents. Conversely, it's also the part of us that makes us see all other men as potential rivals—a burden that can be difficult to control unless we have a good sense of who and what we are.

Sometimes the best way to do that is to maintain our personal simplicity and identity, to know who we are and to stay in the persona we're most comfortable with. While on a personal level the Gen-X phrase "keep it real" makes my teeth hurt, that's really what I think they're talking about—being yourself no matter what they say, to quote Sting. The Red-Bearded Thunderer, Thor, from Nordic mythology, is an excellent example of a god who is extremely gifted at being exactly what he is.

The Tale of Thor and the Midgard-Serpent

It came to pass that Thor and Loki, along with Thor's bondservant Hugi, were journeying in the land of the giants. It came to be night, and they were seeking shelter. They found a building with a great opening at one end, where they rested. In the morning, they were awoken by a great noise—the snoring of the giant Skrymir, whose glove they had slept in!

They traveled with Skrymir, who offered to carry their food in his knapsack. When night came, Skrymir left the sack where they could get their own food, and went to sleep. Try as Thor would, though, he could not open the sack's drawstring. Angry, he struck Skrymir in the head three times while the giant slept, but each time Skrymir complained only of litter and leaves falling from a tree above.

The next day, they arrived at the castle of Utgard-Loki, a great giant king. He dismissed Thor as "small" but then challenged Loki, Thor, and Hugi to contests to prove their greatness.

Loki had soon after lost an eating contest, and Hugi a footrace. It seemed dark for the pride of the Aesir, but then Thor was given his challenges.

He was asked to empty a drinking horn that Utgard-Loki claimed no giant needed more than two draughts to empty. Thor failed in this. He was then asked to pick up Utgard-Loki's cat, and only managed to lift one paw off the ground. Finally, angry, he challenged the giants to a fight and was told he could wrestle Utgard-Loki's old nurse, Elli. Even so, Thor could not defeat the old woman giant, who brought him down to one knee.

With great shame, the Aesir went to sleep. The next day there was much feasting, after which the Aesir took their leave. Utgard-Loki followed them, and there he told them the truth. Loki had lost in an eating contest to the

spirit of fire, and Hugi had failed to outrun a thought.
The drinking horn had had its end in the sea, and Thor
had caused the tides to begin by his valor. The old woman
Elli had been Old Age. And finally, the cat had been the
Midgard-Serpent, the great worm that encircles the earth,
and the giants had been greatly afraid when Thor lifted
one paw off the ground.

It was then that Thor swore he would fight the Ser-
pent one day, and either it or he would be destroyed.

So what is this about, in the long run? Thor is the very personification of strength, of the Warrior, and he knows exactly what it is he can and can't do. He is also offended by tricks and is determined to get that fair fight with the Midgard-Serpent one day. He knows his strengths and his weaknesses, and when someone crosses a line he's drawn—that of expecting a fair fight from his opponent—he decides to take action.

Thor is often a creature of impulse, operating from his gut and heart rather than his head. For all that, the Warrior can be a calculating and deliberate archetype; this is often his modus operandi—a method of operation that, interestingly enough, Thor shares with Loki, his friend, goad, nemesis, and adversary in the Norse myths. Odin's motivations are often veiled and concealed; Thor and Loki, however, share a certain passion and emotional transparency that to me reveals them as brothers under the skin.

Warriors may be complex, but they're rarely convoluted. The Warrior archetype is often the best thing for a man to get in touch with when he knows what he wants, and he wants the strength to go get it. The shadow side of that is that the Warrior's energy can say "take" instead of "get"—and we can cross the line into soldiers, tyrants, and oppressors. This is a difficult balance to maintain and one that frankly we've failed at more than we've succeeded. When accusations, grounded or groundless, are slung at the patriarchy, the primary target is most often this side of the nature of a man. For every explorer, there is a rapist.

If I knew how to solve this, I'd be a minor messiah. All I can do is make one useful generality: the Warrior gets in trouble when he objectifies people. In the Western magickal tradition, one school of thought says that the measure of being a true Adept is to see the Divine in everyone you encounter, no matter who they are or what they're doing at the time. When the Warrior enters his danger zone, he's doing the opposite; he's seeing no one but himself. Everyone else is an obstacle or a source for gratification.[11]

The only counter to this is to remain aware of our emotional natures and transparent to them—to be aware of our shadows. To know what we're doing and why we're doing it. To keep the Warrior under control, a man must remain in touch with his Lover.

And while we're on the subject of emotional transparency, the Warrior is also reflected in a god that I personally

---

11. I have been told by friends and ManKind Project brothers who are involved in substance abuse recovery that this concept is included in most Twelve Step plans. Addicts objectify people and hurt them because other people are not "real." If that's so, what's not to say that acting "manly" (as opposed to acting like a man) is in and of itself an addiction?

think has gotten a bad rep over the centuries. Let's examine the Warrior in his Hellenic embodiment: Ares.

In the words of mythologist Walter Otto (quoted in the work of Jean Shinoda Bolen): "Against this grim spirit of warfare and bloodshed [Ares], the bright form of Athena, stands in admirable contrast, and this contrast is intentional on the part of [Homer]."[12] Of course, Otto is speaking about the portrayal of Ares in Homer's great epic *The Iliad*.

At this point, I cheerily admit that I have an axe to grind here. (I suspect, in keeping with our subject matter, it's bronze.) Yes, the Greeks considered Ares to be the spirit of rapacious bloodlust, the dark side to Athena's oh-so-Hellenic sense of restraint and propriety. To quote Homer directly:

"And flashing-eyed Athene took furious Ares by the hand and spake to him, saying: 'Ares, Ares, thou bane of mortals, thou blood-stained stormer of walls, shall we not now leave the Trojans and Achaeans to fight, to whichsoever of the two it be that father Zeus shall vouchsafe glory?'"[13]

"Bane of mortals." "Blood-stained stormer of walls." Tough language.

To the Romans, however, he was Mars, second only to Jupiter in importance, protector of Romulus and Remus and the Empire. There is a noble side to Ares, a valuable reflection of the Warrior archetype that as men in the twenty-first century we have lost touch with.

---

12. Jean Shinoda Bolen, *Gods in Everyman: A New Psychology of Men's Lives and Loves* (New York: Harper Perennial, 1989), 195.

13. Homer, *The Iliad*, trans. by Samuel Butler (Chicago: Encyclopædia Britannica, 1952). Book XI.

There is a magnificent statue in the Louvre of Ares, nude save an Attic helmet—calm, refined, and yet still deadly. It dates from the High Classical period of Greek history, and in it I see Ares' essential nature—graceful, simple, yet ready at a moment's notice to spring into action and attack or defend as the situation merits. And have no doubt about it: Ares is unquestionably male, a necessary counterpoint to Athena's femininity.

In my own Wiccan tradition, Storyteller Wicca, Ares as Challenger appears at a vital point in our ordination. He is one of the challenges a prospective priest or priestess must pass. I honor Ares; to me, he is the moment between action and reaction, the moment between stasis and change. He is the male desire to move, to act, to change the world—and he is the force and power to make that change reality.

The Tale of Ares as Child and as Father

Ares was the son of Hera and Zeus. While still young, he was imprisoned by the Aloadai, two giants who, because of their great strength and size, had chosen to storm heaven. The Aloadai piled two mountains, Ossa and Pelion, atop each other and attacked the gods atop Olympus, seeking both victory and Hera and Artemis as brides.

They were eventually defeated by the gods and goddesses working in concert, but in that struggle Ares was captured and sealed in a bronze urn where he suffered for thirteen months and came near death. He was only rescued by Hermes after the Aloadai's stepmother told Zeus where to find the young god of war.

> *As he grew older, Ares fathered many children. With Aphrodite he engendered his sons, Phobos and Deimos, as well as the goddess Harmonia, reflecting the harmony between love and war. He also avenged the rape of his daughter, Alcippe, by killing her assailant, a son of Poseidon; entered the fray in the Trojan War against the wishes of Zeus when his son Ascalaphus was killed; and forced Cadmus to serve him for eight years after Cadmus murdered another of his children. This service eventually led to the marriage of Cadmus and Harmonia and the founding of the great city of Thebes.*

Interesting that the "bane of mortals" was that protective of his family, isn't it? It becomes even more convoluted when we realize that Zeus, the father of Ares, didn't really much *like* Ares, and regularly sided with Athena in disputes between Athena and Ares. (Which were, admittedly, legion. Talk about the classic version of sibling rivalry.)

Every man in our society who has transcended a dysfunctional, painful, or broken childhood, or a flawed relationship with a father, to become something more whole has a protector and a god to identify with in Ares. He is the Warrior as self-healer, the man who stops the cycle of abuse. And as that cycle of abuse and self-abuse is one of our greatest challenges as men today, Ares is a vital and potent god to pay honor to—a magickal and powerful symbol of healing, defense, and keeping one's words and obligations.

When men first begin their healing process, it's often awkward, blunt, clumsy. That time of taking the first steps towards emotional literacy occurs when Ares' patronage is the most vital. Let's face it: Ares ain't subtle. He acts rashly at times, his feelings are very widescreen, and he tends to look for the most direct and brutal solution to whatever obstacle he's facing at the time. Men in their first few months of truly feeling—generally after a cathartic experience or intervention—are the same way. Expressing pain is so alien to many of us that a lot of what we do runs off instinct.

That's *okay*. We can hurt people in that state, true, and we must remain constantly aware of our own behavior, but we also are (often for the first time) investing, whole and present, in our own hearts. We are on fire with this new experience—and it's no mistake, perhaps, that Ares is also associated with fire.

This is why it's vital that men not try to go through this process alone. I wrote this book not only to provide a road map for male spirituality and archetype work, but also to bring men together in that work. In my own men's work, the ManKind Project, men continue meeting after the initial weekend experience to check in with each other, to continue to do emotional work, and to keep each other accountable and in integrity about their intentions and desires. I cannot stress how important that work is. All the Arean desire to protect one's family and to express pain is greatly crippled without other men to help us maintain our boundaries in the face of change.

As with all virtues, though, keeping one's obligations and defending one's family has its shadow—and there may be no greater example of that than the tale of Gawain, the

Perfect Knight whose death came because of his desire for revenge.

However, we're going to take a side trip first into the murky world of mythopoetic interpretation. Let's be blunt; the Arthurian myth cycle is a confusing mishmash, reinterpreted over hundreds of years by authors who usually had an agenda of one sort or another, stealing characters from other tales and adding them with great glee. For example, the first Arthurian stories show up in Geoffrey of Monmouth's *Historia Regum Brittaniae*, written around 1135—but not until around the year 1200 did we get such small pieces of the Arthurian cycle as Camelot, the Round Table, and Lancelot du Lac, courtesy of French poet Chrétien de Troyes.[14]

In short, the gods themselves, armed with heavy weapons and an army of trained scribes, could not make a coherent single interpretation of the story of the King of the Britons. I'm not even going to try. This is an interpretation I like; if you don't like it, write down your carefully researched refutation in triplicate and then make three paper airplanes.

Ahem. That said . . .

Gawain is one of the oldest, if not the oldest, figures in Arthurian myth. He first appears in "Culhwch and Olwen," one of the tales from the Welsh myth cycle *The Mabinogion*, where he was known as Gwalchmei, the "Hawk of May." While some of the figures in "Culhwch" are familiar—Arthur,

---

14. Arthurian information taken from "Timeless Myths: Arthurian Legends," www.timelessmyths.com/arthurian/index.html, and "King Arthur & the Knights of the Round Table," www.kingarthursknights.com. (Both websites accessed May 29, 2007).

Kei, Bedwyr (Bedivere), Gwenhwyfar—Gwalchmei, while being one of Arthur's advisors and knights, is almost a divine figure, a solar deity like Lugh, son of the goddess Gwyar.

As for his skill, well . . .

> Gwalchmei had also [been] compared with the greatest Irish hero, Cu Chulainn, who was the son of the solar god Lugh. In the tale of Culhwch and Olwen, Gwalchmei was the hero who "never returned without fulfilling his quest." Gwalchmei was also the best walker and rider.[15]

Or, in the words of Lady Charlotte Guest's translation of *The Mabinogion*:

> He called Gwalchmai the son of Gwyar, because he never returned home without achieving the adventure of which he went in quest. He was the best of footmen and the best of knights. He was nephew to Arthur, the son of his sister, and his cousin.[16]

In short, this early version of Gawain was the perfect knight. So how did we get from this to . . .

The Tale of the Death of Sir Gawain

> It was toward the end of the dream that was Camelot, after the Quest of the Grail was completed. Many good knights had been slain, and Sir Mordred and Sir Agra-

---

15. "Gawain: the Solar God" at "Timeless Myths: Arthurian Legends," www .timelessmyths.com/arthurian/roundtable.html#Solar. (accessed May 29, 2007).

16. *The Mabinogion*, trans. by Lady Charlotte Guest (London: Quartich, 1877).

vaine had told King Arthur of the unfaithfulness of his queen Guinevere.

As the law commanded, Arthur attempted to put his wife to death by burning—but Lancelot rescued her, and in the process Gawain's brothers Gareth and Gaheris were slain.

Now Gawain had remained true to Arthur, and it was he who counseled war to be done upon Lancelot. Arthur, Gawain, and the remaining knights of Arthur's court made war upon Lancelot, and only the grace of the Pope made them cease. Yet still Gawain was angry and sorrowing over his dead brothers, so with his counsel and that of the traitor Mordred did Arthur and Lancelot never make peace again nor return to their friendship as before.

And in the fighting between Gawain and Lancelot, Gawain was sorely wounded—for Gawain was never the equal of Lancelot du Lac, try though he would to equal him. For Gawain's strength would rise until the sun was highest in the sky, then fail him in the afternoon and evening. And Gawain was forced to withdraw.

As Thomas of Malory said, "And Sir Gawaine evermore calling him traitor knight, and said: 'Wit thou well Sir Launcelot, when I am whole I shall do battle with thee again, for I shall never leave thee till that one of us be slain.'"[17]

And soon after this, Gawain was wounded sorely when the traitor Mordred claimed the throne and was

---

17.   Sir Thomas Malory, *Le Morte d'Arthur* (New York: E. P. Dutton, 1923). Book XX, chapter XXII.

removed through force of arms. And as he had not recov-
ered from the wound he had taken at Benwick, he died in
Arthur's arms—and soon after came the tragic day when
Arthur fell with neither Lancelot nor Gawain at his side,
and the kingdom was lost.

From a historical viewpoint, it's easy to see what happened here. Gwalchmei and "Culhwch and Olwen" date from around 1100; *Le Morte d'Arthur* was written sometime between 1450 and 1470 while Malory was in debtor's prison. Although most of the changes can be put down to the Gallicization and Christianization of the text, there's still some essential shift in Gawain's character.

I think I can put it in one word: revenge.

Gawain is obsessed with revenge. Most of his later actions in the late versions of the Arthurian cycle come from his desire to avenge one or another of his dead brothers (which do admittedly seem to be legion; apparently the medieval chroniclers thought Morgause, Arthur's sister, had children in litters). At times he seems petty, spiteful, and childish, snarling quietly to himself that Lancelot is better than he is—and when the Guinevere-shaped chink in Lancelot's armor finally manifests, Gawain is right there to try to drive his sword into it. Malory even seems to admit Gawain has been a bit of a jerk; at his death, he gives him a scene where he writes a letter to Lancelot, apologizing for his behavior and begging Lancelot to come to the rescue of Camelot and Arthur. (Lancelot does come, but he is too late.)

Revenge is a human emotion, too, but men are often obsessive about having the wrongs done them avenged. This is a common literary and cinematic device, but more tragic is the ubiquitous impulse to "get someone back" that starts in grade school and for many men never lets up. In my experience, it takes two forms: either a man is trying somehow to be the agent of karmic recompense, making someone pay for their sins, or else it's a more primal desire to get the son of a bitch who got you.

Either way, we are looking at a destructive impulse. I do not know of anyone who's big and bad enough to be a personal agent of karma unless karma intends them to be so—and if it happens that way, well, it's not something you have to work at much. I've known—heck, I've *been*—the guy who wants to "get the son of a bitch." From flame wars to Pagan politics, I have a long and rather depressing history of being right in the middle. Finally, about seven years ago, I got out of it; I had a good personal example and I think I'd finally grown enough that I could move past it.

Imagine my surprise when once I did that, the past actions of the people I was angry at caught up with them without any help from me. It was, frankly, gratifying.

I can't guarantee that will happen for you. But if Gawain teaches us a lesson, it's that our interpretation of what we need to avenge may be lacking. There may be a bigger picture, or we may just need to get the heck out of the way.

The two sides of the coin are a lesson for all of us to learn. Gwalchmei is the greatest knight because he doesn't give in to his shadow; Gawain revels in it, and eventually he pays the ultimate price.

For Further Thought

Do I operate on impulse or control?

Am I allowing my own healing? And am I damaging other people in doing it?

Am I acting out of strength, or out of revenge or personal interest?

MAGICKAL WORKING

Initiating a Life Change

Before we begin, a little explanation as to what this means:

When I say "life change," I mean something deeply resonant on an emotional, mental, or psychic level. This would be a working you would do before coming out of the closet, adopting a child, entering rehab, joining the Peace Corps—save this one for any action that will change your entire life.

That said, please also be aware that magick is not a substitute for competent outside help. If you're considering entering rehab, seek out professional advice. If you're coming out of the closet—either the traditional one dealing with sexual orientation or the broom closet of religion—make sure you have supportive friends around you. If you're joining the Peace Corps, get your shots.

Also—and this can resonate with the Gawain portion of the chapter—this is a useful working for getting rid of a desire for revenge. Doing so can be a way of calling on the energy of the Warrior to allow us to let go; we can choose to put down our shields as well as take them up.

Recommended Tools

- A shield: a metal or plastic disk, unmarked. If you can get or make a toy kite shield with no design on it, so much the better.
- A sword: a small dagger or boot knife
- Paints, markers, whatever art supplies you like working with and find crafty
- Face paint, if desired
- A red candle

Light your smudge and call the directions (page 262).

With the room as dark as possible, say the following:

I stand surrounded by darkness. With the help of the Warrior, he who guards and guides, I will strike a new light in my life.

Light the candle at this time. Take your face paints and paint your face with as little or as much war paint as you want. (Yes, you may feel silly at first. But men have been wearing body paint for thousands of years, and when you do it, you put on a different face with which to face the world. In the case of this working, that's a vital thought to keep in mind; you're putting on a different face on the outside to change the inside.)

Lay your shield and sword out before you. Chant, sing, or breathe as you wish, concentrating on the change that you're going to make in your life, while you take your art supplies and make designs on your shield. It doesn't matter if the symbols are particularly artistic; what matters is that you see a relationship between the symbols and the reality you are evoking. When you are finished, lay the sword and shield in front of you and say:

> *I stand blessed by light. This sword and this shield are the emblems of my life's present challenge. They will defend me and fill me with the energy of the Warrior, and it is my will that I make this change in my life. So long as I remember my sword and shield, I shall remain victorious* (or, you can say: *free of my desire for revenge*). *In the name of the God, so mote it be!*

While the candle is still burning, put the sword and shield in a safe place. Extinguish the candle and sit in darkness, meditating on this change in your life. When you are done, thank the directions and ancestors and close the rite.

RITUAL OF AFFIRMATION

Accepting the Quest

Joseph Campbell in his expression of the Hero's Journey says the first step is the Call to Adventure, the moment when the youth is told or realizes for the first time that he has reached a point at which everything in his life is changing, when he has discovered his own moment of initiation and the challenges he will face in becoming initiated.

This ritual is designed to honor the moment when a man accepts his Call to Adventure, and sets forth to achieve his personal quest and retrieve his grail.

This ceremony should include a circle of men, including, if possible, one man of around twenty (the Youth), one around thirty-five (the Warrior), one around fifty (the King), and one around seventy (the Elder). A simple altar should be laid, with a God and Goddess candle, quarter candles, and symbols of the elements: a wand, a blade, a cup, and a stone.

The candidate should enter the circle as unadorned as possible; if he is comfortable with it and the other men in the circle are comfortable with it, ritual nudity[18] is acceptable for this rite. The candidate should carry one sacred object that he would consider worth swearing an oath to the Warrior archetype on: a blade, a talisman, something that speaks to that energy for him.[19]

Warrior: You step into this circle with a sacred quest that you desire other men bear witness to. Not everyone steps into this circle; not all men have a single sacred quest that will drive their days, and there is no shame in one man having one and another man not. Yet you have one melody that sings to you strong enough to shape your entire life, at least at this stage of your life, and you have chosen to swear an oath before your brothers and the gods. At this time, what is the quest you will follow?

---

18. Oh gods, here we go. The ritual nudity question. I'm no fashion plate. I am, in fact, somewhat fat and have hair on my back. I'm not going to appear nude for the sake of aesthetics. I also know that sometimes nudity is a valuable part of my spiritual practice. If it bugs you, don't do it. But do, if you have time and energy, look at *why* it bugs you. You may find something worth examining underneath. If minors are involved in any way, do not use ritual nudity.

19. I have known some pretty diverse examples of warrior talismans. Homemade chain mail, WWII-vintage machetes, katanas and wakizashis, automatic pistols (unloaded), sword canes, quarterstaves, bamboo practice swords . . . whatever says "honor," "guardianship," and "responsibility" to you will work.

Candidate speaks of his quest in his own words.

The candidate is brought to the center of the circle, before the altar. Each of the four officiants takes his place in the appropriate direction.

Youth: I call to the East, the spirits of Air! At dawn, the great Quest begins, the knight setting forth under the rising sun. Hail and welcome, spirits of the East, essence of Air!

Warrior: I call to the South, the spirits of Fire! As the sun rises to its highest point, the great Quest continues, the knight riding at his apex of power. Hail and welcome, spirits of the South, essence of Fire!

King: I call to the West, the spirits of Water! As the sun sets, the great Quest is completed, the wanderer riding to hearth and home. Hail and welcome, spirits of the West, essence of Water!

Elder: I call to the North, the spirits of Earth! In the darkest hour, the quester considers his lessons, and passes his wisdom on to those who will quest after him. Hail and welcome, spirits of the North, essence of Earth!

Youth: We welcome the Great Goddess: Maiden, Mother, Crone, She whose favor we seek on the field of our individual challenges. Without the one, there cannot be the other. Hail, Great Goddess!

Elder: We welcome the Great God, king, warrior, magician, lover, He who inspires courage. Without the one, there cannot be the other. Hail, Great God!

The men stand in a circle around the quester.

Youth: I have heard your quest, and I witness it. My counsel is to seek joy in it. Remember to laugh, to cry, to feel, and to live to your fullest. You must be the master of your quest; do not let it master you so that you forget to live.

Warrior: I have heard your quest, and I witness it. My counsel is to have courage. You may meet challenges, obstacles, or adversaries; should you know who you are, nothing can stand against you. There is no enemy in the world but yourself. Accept help when offered, bravely and without ego.

King: I have heard your quest, and I witness it. My counsel is to question. Always consider whether the actions you take are the best actions for your success. Be willing to think outside the box. Be willing to walk the road less traveled.

Elder: I have heard your quest, and I witness it. My counsel is to know when it is over. The greatest folly of a man is often that he remains clinging to things after their time has gone by. Know when to say enough and to lay down your sword.

Youth: You have been given counsel. Do you still wish to set forth on this your quest, knowing that before you lies low points, challenges, trials, and thresholds to be crossed?

Candidate responds.

King: Then, [*name*], we witness your self-declaration as a seeker and a follower of your personal quest. May you find what you seek.

Elder: As an Elder of our tribe, I commend to you the watchword of the Warrior: *courage.* It is not being without fear, but moving forward in the Great Work of manhood despite fear. Let it always be your shield.

Warrior: *(lays hand on forehead)* I bless you in the name of the Warrior.

King: *(to the directions as he speaks)* The Earth of determination, the Water of love, the Fire of the spirit, and the Air of wisdom; we thank and bless their spirits, knowing they are with us always. May they guide you on your quest.

Youth: We thank the Great Goddess, She who is our other soul, for standing with us tonight.

Elder: We thank the Great God, He who is our root and our spirit, for standing with us tonight.

Warrior: Go now and begin your journey. We are with you always. Come to us should you need our wisdom. We are your brothers.

VI

THE TRICKSTER

LOOKS CAN BE DECEIVING

*The first principle is that you must not fool yourself—
and you are the easiest person to fool.*

—Richard Feynman,
Caltech commencement address, 1974

A h, sweet relief as I'm writing this. See, the last two chapters were hard to write. This one is going to be easy. Everyone can figure out the Trickster, right? Call him Rafiki, Br'er Rabbit, Coyote, whatever you like—he's simple. Basic. Uncomplicated. Everyone gets him. He comes along, dispenses cosmic and comic wisdom, whaps you upside the head with something handy (like, say, a '73 Studebaker[20]), and then moves on. If he's not doing that, he's taking someone who's too serious and a little slow and making him look like an absolute fool.

No problem. We all understand this archetype. Let's move on to the next chapter.

brief pause for ironic comedy

Yeah, *right*.

If you've been paying attention, you've seen in my Ritual of Affirmation sections that each archetype has a watchword, a central theme that can be expressed in a single thought. Does it confuse you to know the Trickster's watchword is *truth*? It sure confused me until I figured it out. It is often the

---

20. Are you going to tell the Coyote they didn't make Studebakers in 1973? Go right ahead. I'll be waiting. Over there. In the blast shelter.

Trickster's purpose in life to point out the truth behind the illusions that we as men maintain: illusions of power, grandeur, standing, confidence, strength. This is dimly reflected in the concept of the historical court jester, the one man who could poke fun at a king. But while the court jester was often a pathetic figure, the Trickster stands in his strength and calls it like he sees it. When we are pompous and overblown, somewhere there's Trickster energy holding a very large hatpin, ready to perform an emergency concussive deflation. We may not like it at the time, but it could save our lives.

I speak from experience. I admit it; I have in my life been terribly pompous and self-important. I still slip into it occasionally until someone in my life—usually either my beloved Elisabeth or a ManKind Project brother—calls me out on it.

That kind of all-knowing, all-powerful attitude is one of the pitfalls that men face in modern society. We are programmed to have all the answers, and expected to always be serious and keep our head. We don't get to laugh much, and we are almost never allowed to laugh at ourselves. Given those circumstances, is it any wonder that we need Trickster energy?

We must, however, keep track of what the Trickster is *not*. The Trickster is not a buffoon or a village idiot; there is usually some serious content behind what he does, some greater purpose. This isn't always true—sometimes Tricksters are just Tricksters—but it usually applies. The Trickster is not a fool, a simple comedic foil like Chaplin in *Modern Times*; he is neither helpless nor a victim of circumstances. And above all, the Trickster is rarely if ever merciful. He can be compassionate, feeling the pain of those he instructs—but like Rafiki in *The Lion King*, he will still whack you in the head hard, usually chirping, "Ah, yes, the past hurts, doesn't it?"

And sometimes the Trickster will guard your life.

The Tale of Bes the Protector

He was never an "official" god of Egypt, with great temples and priests who were the confidants of Pharaohs. He was probably even an import from further south in Africa, not truly Egyptian at all, not in the beginning. Even at the height of his worship, during the rule of the Ptolemies, he merited only a room in a dwelling, perhaps used for birthings or healing rituals.

He is the god of music, dance, laughter, and beer. He guards children as they are born, encouraging them to take the next step on the great dance of life. When a child laughs or smiles at something no one else can see, it is said the ugly dwarf-god Bes —for so he is portrayed, an ugly dwarf with a ridiculous grimace—is making funny faces for the baby.

Yet . . . when snakes were driven into homes due to the rising of the Nile, it was Bes who was invoked to protect the family. It was his responsibility to fight off evil demons at birthings. His face was often portrayed as part lion, and his name may relate to the Nubian word besa, which means both "cat" and "protector." And almost alone among Egyptian gods, he was portrayed full-face rather than in profile. Why? No one is sure. But Ellen Cannon Reed, follower of both Wicca and the Egyptian

deities, believed that Bes had a hidden side—that of a
guardian who protects us during our darkest moments.

Bes is a great manifestation of the Trickster as the spirit of
laughter—laughter at ourselves, laughter with others, laughter at darkness. The one thing that evil cannot abide is mock-
ery, laughter, satire, or parody; it requires entirely too much
self-importance to be evil to ever allow oneself to laugh. (Evil
laughter such as the classic "MU-HA-HA-HA-HA!" doesn't
count. I don't know what that is, but it's not humor.)

As Reed puts it:

[A] good friend who was a registered nurse recalled a
time . . . when she and others were working frantically to
keep a two-year-old child alive.

As the tension built, as they worked harder and
harder, the jokes started. It was terrible and obscene dark
humor . . . The jokes kept [the doctors and nurses] from
screaming.[21]

That is the lesson of Bes, that often the only thing we have
holding us together is our ability to laugh. What we want to
do in those situations, what we're hardwired to do as human
beings, is to collapse into our own fear, babbling softly and
curling up in a fetal position. I know that it's what *I* want to do.
Instead, as men, our grace, our gift is to step up. We respond,
we step up, and we become heroes in our own quiet way.

Bes also teaches us to laugh just for the sake of laughter—not nasty laughter or mean laughter, but joyous, soul-

---

21.   Ellen Cannon Reed, *Circle of Isis: Ancient Egyptian Magick for Modern Witches*
      (Franklin Lakes, NJ: New Page Books, 2002), 78.

cleansing, triumphant laughter. I have seen men who in a moment of triumph gave forth a great joyful shout that often trailed off into laughter. I have laughed through tears at seeing another man achieve something great. Yet we don't often laugh when we're just being us, or if we do it's because we're laughing at something. We certainly don't laugh at ourselves very often; we're too serious and powerful to allow *that* sort of thing. There is, in fact, a subtle societal indoctrination to not laugh at ourselves: "Wipe that grin off your face." "Aren't you ever serious?" "Do you think this is a joke?"

For me, this lesson is especially potent. We need to remember to laugh at ourselves, so that we can express other emotions in a healthy, positive manner. Sometimes when we laugh, we can find power within ourselves. This is an incredibly potent truth, and a truth that we as men often completely miss.

An equally important truth about Bes is that Tricksters are often defenders in disguise. The most popular Trickster archetype in the twentieth century is probably my personal patron saint, Bugs Bunny. Ever noticed that no matter how he's being attacked—Elmer's trying to shoot him, Yosemite Sam is trying to shoot him, Daffy's trying to get him shot in "wabbit season!"—he rarely, if ever, responds with force of his own. (There are a few exceptions, true, but they're almost all against one-time villains like the "one lump or two?" lion—perhaps they don't earn the respect of Bugs enough to matter.) Bugs is almost a pacifist most of the time—and it's only when his anger gets the better of him that things go wrong.

I've talked about the subtle indoctrination in our society to never laugh at ourselves. Many men would be much healthier if they realized that almost everything we encounter has a joke hidden in it—and a lesson, and a sorrow, and a way to reach out to others. When we realize that nothing occurs without a reason, and nothing exists without joy and sorrow and wisdom all intermixed in it, we become fully alive and embrace our emotions and our power. And when we do—all sorts of amazing things are possible.

The Tale of Sun Wukong and Sanzang

Sun Wukong, the Monkey King, was born from a stone and was noted for his bravery, strength, and cleverness. In time, he became sad that he was mortal, and through study and practice of the arcane arts he became skilled and gained many mystical items of power. Finally, he ate the peaches of Mother Wang, the Queen Mother of Heaven, and gained immortality.

Sun was very brave, but his infuriating and trouble-making nature eventually led Heaven to make war on him after his many thefts and tricks. He was finally tricked in turn by the Buddha, who imprisoned him.

Sun was released when he offered to accompany Sanzang, the priest who was destined to bring the Buddhist Sutras to China, on his journey to retrieve those scriptures. Sun was tricked into wearing a magickal band to control his behavior while he sought atonement guiding the wise priest.

Many supernatural beings tried to stop Sanzang from bringing wisdom to China, and the group faced eighty-one tribulations in their search for the Sutras. But once

they were retrieved and brought triumphantly to China,
Sun Wukong was named a Buddha.

Let's see: you start life as a monkey, steal immortality, make war on Heaven, steal stuff from the Jade Emperor, and still get made a Buddha. That strikes me as a heck of a career curve.

I admit it: the story of Sun Wukong is one of my favorite stories. One of my best friends is a devotee of his—I'm not going to say follower. I suspect trying to follow Sun Wukong would get you pelted with bananas—and my friend's life is never boring. I've watched him grow and change over more than ten years, and finally come back into a place where he has become a questing Knight, making his own way on his Hero's Journey. (I'm proud of him, too. He was the first man I brought to the work of the ManKind Project after my first weekend.)

Just like my friend Ilari, Sun Wukong is a great example of the hero hiding behind the Trickster. (See a theme here? Good. You're paying attention.) When our archetypical energies are in balance, we are capable of shifting from one to another—fluid, elegant, all finally leading to the divine majesty of the Elder. But that rarely happens without work. Being a hero and still keeping one's sense of humor, joy, and wonder in the world is delicate work; too often, heroes see the evil in the world and then are consumed by it. The world becomes grimmer, darker, less miraculous. Sun Wukong, despite eventually becoming a Buddha, maintained his incorrigibility: balance in all things, which reflects his Buddha nature. In the words of Oscar Wilde, who is often quoted in the work of my coven, Thalia Clan: "Life is too important to be taken seriously."

In modern life, men become out of balance in their archetypical energies, and often the part that suffers the most is the Trickster. When he is allowed to manifest, it's like Spring Break gone horribly wrong—drugs, alcohol, irresponsible behavior, and eventually someone, or multiple someones, get hurt. We spend so much time chaining the Trickster down—chaining down our ability to laugh, to be sneaky and irresponsible and fun-loving and, yes, occasionally infuriating—that when the Trickster breaks out, very bad things happen.

Sometimes, when the chains break, all light goes away.

The Tale of Loki and the Death of Baldur

Loki is the blood brother of Odin, ruler of the Norse gods. He is the son of a Giant and a God, and as such often has to balance his dual allegiances. Nevertheless, his blood-brotherhood with Odin has brought him into Asgard, the land of the gods, and has given him a high position among the Aesir.

Loki is a trickster and a most cunning god, a wizard of renown and an accomplished shapeshifter. Whenever things are darkest, Loki will have the solution—even if he caused the problem by his own desire to make trouble in the first place. Having heritage of both giant and god, he has access to magickal powers that few, if any, of the Aesir have, and his dualist worldview means that he often slips from woe to weal and back to woe without any warning. Thor barely tolerates him, and it is only Loki's relationship with Odin that saves his neck time and time again.

Yet the story is told that Loki turns to darkness. A prophecy foreordains that Baldur, the god of Light, will die at the beginning of Ragnarök, the time of the end of the world. His mother Frigga, the queen of the gods and the wife of Odin, obtains a promise from every living thing not to harm Baldur, but she overlooks the mistletoe because she thinks it harmless.

The gods gather and playfully begin to throw objects at Baldur, proving his invincibility. As steel and oak refuse to harm him, Loki changes shape to that of an old woman and asks Frigga if all things will truly not harm Baldur. Finding out about the mistletoe, Loki fashions a dart of the plant and gives it to Hod, the blind half-brother of Baldur, to throw. Baldur is slain.

Bereft, Frigga asks Hel, the goddess of the underworld, to give Baldur back. Hel responds that she will only do so if all living things weep for Baldur—and when Loki in human disguise refuses to weep, Baldur stays with Hel.

On a personal basis, I've always had trouble with this part of Norse mythology. First of all, the tale of Ragnarök has always seemed to be sort of an attachment, never quite feeling right. In general, Pagans don't go in for end-of-the-world scenarios;[22] we leave that to followers of other faiths and Jerry Bruckheimer.

---

22. One school of belief is that the Ragnarök myth cycle, which first appeared in the poem "Völuspá," written around 1000, was a tool used by Christian missionaries in Iceland to gain converts. This theory, first proposed by Sigurður Nordal in 1979, has some adherence among Pagan scholars, including yours truly—although there are just as many, if not more, theorists who say it belongs there.

However, if we ignore the context of Loki's behavior and just examine the behavior itself, it's still pretty clear there are some serious issues going on here. In Norse mythology, Loki is the perpetual outsider, the figure who never quite fits in. He bridges two worlds, not fitting into either one—and he channels his feelings about that into occasional bouts of destructiveness. In many ways, Loki is the perfect example of what Moore and Gillette call the High Chair Tyrant:

> *The High Chair Tyrant is . . . the center of the Universe . . .*
>
> *[He] may continue to be a ruling archetypal influence in adulthood. We all know the story of the promising leader . . . who starts to rise to great prominence and then . . . sabotages his success, and crashes to the earth.*[23]

In the Ragnarökian interpretation of Loki, it's all about Loki, and as soon as he crosses the line and is imprisoned—taken out of the limelight of being Odin's faithful sidekick—he fully embraces the darkness within himself and leads the forces of destruction at Ragnarök. He unravels all creation, just as Moore and Gillette say; he "crashes to the earth," and the earth is taken with him to succumb to the icy grip of Fimbulwinter.

We all know men who have fallen into the grip of this shadow—men who have overreached their bounds or let their elevated status go to their heads. One of the greatest dangers a man can become victim to is the belief that the Universe revolves around him and that the rules are different

---

23. Moore and Gillette, *King, Warrior, Magician, Lover* (San Francisco: HarperSan-Francisco, 1991), 24.

for him. In the ManKind Project, we call this "special boy" energy; it's the High Chair Tyrant at work, hogging center stage and demanding that he be the exception to the rule.

This is the pitfall of Trickster energy—the desire to be the center of attention and the anger when that desire is thwarted. Again, it's a situation out of balance; sometimes it's best to not be in the limelight when your latest prank goes really, really right (or horribly wrong—either one can be funny). As in all archetypes, the Trickster is one of many faces, and care must be taken to make sure he gets his fair share of energy—but *only* his fair share.

For Further Thought

Am I in need of a concussive deflation?

Are my energies in balance? Can I shift from Trickster to Hero without a hitch?

Am I demanding to be the center of attention?

MAGICKAL WORKING

Clearing Away Personal Illusions

At some point, most men come to a place where they realize that they've been operating under false data and false views of self. Popular culture dismisses this glibly as the "midlife crisis" or a "crisis of faith." If the culture responds to it at all, it makes fun of the situation, making sly digs at buying a new sports car or finding a younger mistress.

Here's some food for thought: if, say, a TV sitcom made the same snide comments about menopause that it makes about this time of transition, what do you suppose the response would be?

Recommended Tools

- Advertisements. Specifically, pictures of the things that make up your illusory life: fast cars, liquor, pictures of women as objects, whatever makes up the illusions you would like to surround yourself with to keep from dealing with the real issues

- A white candle

- Glue

- A sheet of heavy paper

- A photo of yourself; the more you look like the person those advertisements would like you to be, the better. If your midlife crisis is truly midlife, use a photo of yourself taken when you were younger

Light your smudge and call the directions (page 262).

Light the white candle, meditating on the concept of truth. What does truth mean to you? If you have any feelings about the subject of truth, any fear about facing your truth, allow yourself to feel it.

Lay out the sheet of paper in front of you and glue your picture precisely in the center. Say the following:

This is my illusory life. I am surrounded by my illusions,
by what other people want to manipulate me into needing,
wanting, having to have.

Then, thoughtfully and in silence, paste the other pictures around you. Make a collage. Be as elegant or as basic as you want. This isn't about artistic talent; it's about creating potent symbols that resonate with you.

When you have finished, set the collage down and meditate on it for a long moment. Then say:

These are my illusions. I am surrounded by what other people think I need to have, how I need to act, who I need to be. I am defined as a consumer, an image, a stereotype, rather than as a man.

I choose to dispel my illusions and deny my false definitions. I choose to embrace truth. I take joy in my truth, embracing my inner fire and laughter. I am who I will to be, in the name of the Trickster, he who laughs at those who take themselves too seriously.

Meditate on the energy of laughter—heck, if you have an urge to do so, laugh! Then place the collage in a safe place where you can refer to it. Should you need support or a reminder of what you don't want in your life, refer to it.

When the collage is no longer needed—and you'll know when that is—you can burn it, bury it, or cast it into running water (but don't pollute).

RITUAL OF AFFIRMATION

Atoning for the Wrong

Yes, I said atonement.

I realize that for most Pagans atonement isn't a popular concept. After all, groveling and making a great production of our sins is what many of us left behind, right?

That is true. But the fact remains that all of us make mistakes. We're human, we have shadows, we screw up. If we wrong someone, it's easy and glib to say "karma will take care of it," when frankly what we need to do sometimes is heal the rift we have with another. If I hurt someone, the last thing they want to hear me doing is ignoring my personal responsibility and babbling about karma. The hard truth is this: the Law of Three, or what goes around comes around, or whatever you want to call it, does not heal human relationships. No one was ever forgiven because their karma caught up with them. Forgiveness must be asked for, so that reconciliation can occur.

While this ritual does include a circle of men as witnesses, its guidance and moderation is the province of an Elder of the men's community.

The candidate enters the circle of men in silence, and remains silent except for specific parts in the ritual where he is asked to speak. There is no altar; the only ritual trapping is a dark stone, perhaps the size of an egg. Other than being dark-colored, the only requirement for the stone is that its weight be noticeable in the hand.

The Elder turns and looks at each man in the circle.

> **Elder:** In this sacred space, a man is going to speak of a wrong he has committed that weighs on his soul. The shadow of our inner selves can be a dark and shameful thing. To remain in this circle, you must swear that what is said, seen, and done here will remain here. If you cannot swear this oath, I charge you to leave the circle. Do you so swear?
>
> *The Elder then gets a verbal acknowledgement of this oath from each man in turn.*
>
> **Elder:** We welcome the elements: Air, Earth, Fire, Water, and the inner space of the self.

All Men: Welcome.

Elder: We welcome the great Goddess, our other half.

All Men: Welcome.

Elder: We welcome the great God, who watches over our rites.

All Men: Welcome.

The Elder offers the candidate the stone.

Elder: You have stepped into this circle of your brothers in order to own a shadow. Will you accept this burden and name your wrong?

At this time, the candidate speaks. This part is, necessarily, free-form; the only guideline is that the candidate is encouraged by the circle of men, interjecting if necessary, to keep the details of what he says focused on himself. If he broke his word to another man, for example, keep the candidate focused on what part of himself led to the breaking of that oath.

It is possible that this circle has been called for a man to acknowledge some deep wrong from his past that he needs to bring out and heal. In all things, this circle is brought together not to condemn or judge the man, but to help him heal his shadow. Hold the man if he cries, offer him help if he's angry—that's what you're there for.

When it seems the man is finished:

Elder: You have stated your wrong. What part of it is related to the illusions and shadows you hold in yourself?

Again, let the man speak. When he is finished:

Elder: You have been handed a stone, a portion of the Mother of the earth and the Father of the mountains. It is dark, symbolizing your shadow.

Will you bear it until you have made recompense to the one you have wronged or, if that is not possible, to yourself?

Candidate responds.

Elder: You men assembled here in this circle, will you help this man stay aware of his illusions?

Circle responds.

Elder: Then I commend to you this wisdom: no one can forgive you until you forgive yourself. Consider this, and return the stone to me when you are finished with recompense and forgiveness. As an Elder of our tribe, I commend to you the watchword of the Trickster: *truth.* Keep your truth firmly in mind and illusions become just that.

Elder: *(to the directions as he speaks)* The Earth of determination, the Water of love, the Fire of the spirit, and the Air of wisdom: we thank and bless their spirits, knowing they are with us always. May they guide you on your quest.

We thank the Great Goddess, She who is our other soul, for standing with us tonight.

We thank the Great God, He who is our root and our spirit, for standing with us tonight.

Go now, and begin your journey. We are with you always. Come to us should you need our wisdom. We are your brothers.

VII

THE GREEN MAN
FEELING THE CYCLE TURN

As we look deeply within, we understand our perfect balance. There is no fear of the cycle of birth, life, and death. For when you stand in the present moment, you are timeless.

—Rodney Yee

One of the most commonly celebrated archetypes of the God today is that of the Green Man. Interestingly enough, the Green Man is also a very old symbol; churches all over Britain and Europe have his face—wise, thoughtful, enigmatic, perhaps a little alien, staring out from stonework all around. Nowadays, you can head into any garden store and take home a plaster Green Man to hang by your birdbath or on your porch. He has quietly become omnipresent in a world where his woods are cut down every day to build yet another subdivision.

However, his ancestry is muddled. First named by Lady Raglan in a folklore journal in 1939, he may have been a symbol of Christian suffering caught in the trap of nature and this world.

As a society, we have honored the Apollonian virtues of order, control, hierarchy, and restraint for hundreds of years. This has, however, resulted in our being distant from the natural world, seeing ourselves as no longer part of it; and since we are not part of it, we are free to abuse it, exploit it, and crush it under the boots of our soldiers and our empires.

The Green Man is the emerging counter to that. Far from being a pacifistic, lighthearted fey figure, he is the warrior of the greenwood, the avenger of that same exploitation and distance. He is unabashedly and unashamedly male, unstintingly powerful, but still compassionate to his children, so long as they remember that they, too, are part of the cycle of life, of creation, of the primal joy of forest and field.

In the words of Dr. Dan Noel: "We have needed a Father Nature for a long time, and never more urgently than now, when all over the planet, armored men, in or out of uniform, terrorize each other, women and children, and what remains of the wildwood."[24]

My own work with the ManKind Project has taught me in great detail the difference between a soldier and a warrior: a soldier takes orders, but a warrior makes his own way. The Green Man is definitely a warrior. His cause is that of defending the cycle of the grain and the wood and the seasons. Like any warrior, he is not benevolent to those who harm his charges; like any man, he may take action with a fierce and determined mien. The Green Man is not a caricature of Mother Nature in drag; he is deep and primal and unchained. He is Father Nature, a symbol we can cling to as we try to redefine exactly what a man is.

The Green Man is also known as the Horned Lord, a symbol that is unimaginably ancient. While in his horned guise, the Green Man's most common portrayals date from the first few centuries before the beginning of the Christian era (most notably the time of the Gundestrup cauldron), but

---

24. Dr. Dan Noel, "Common Themes, East & West: The Green Man," mythinglinks .org/ct~greenmen~DanNoel.html. Originally published in the *Santa Barbara Independent*, June 13–20, 2002, 25–26 (accessed May 29, 2007).

horned figures of power and mystery have been found in Paleolithic cave paintings that are over 40,000 years old.

The Green Man is such an old figure, in fact, that we can tell little about him historically. While there are a few archaeological details about Cernunnos, we have no myths or stories about him. As such, modern Wiccans have taken his name and applied it to the Horned God of Wiccan cosmology. While I'm not saying that Cernunnos in Roman times was honored and viewed the same way modern Wiccans view the Horned Lord, it is the modern version of the god that we will consider.

The Tale of the Horned Lord

This is the mystery—the Lady is eternal, the Lord is not and yet is.

In spring, he is the Horned Lord. He rampages through spring, untrammeled and primal. He is the spirit of the wood, the spirit of growth, the spirit of every rampant seed and sapling.

At Beltane, he will marry the Lady. At Midsummer, he will impregnate her, and some say that he will meet with the Queen of Faerie on that same night and the Queen will show him his fate. On Lammas, he will be slain, guaranteeing the harvest, while the gathered people cry, "John Barleycorn must die!"

In spring, though, he is invincible, immortal, powerful. He runs with the stag; he wrestles with bears; he knows the secrets the rabbits tell in their burrows. He can hear the oak and rowan sing as they stretch their branches towards the sun.

> *At Mabon, he will be mourned as the harvest comes in. At Samhain, he will throw open the gates of the underworld and return, allowing the Honored Dead to return themselves for one night. At Yule, he will be reborn as his own child, the Sun Child. At Imbolc, he will come into the first of his power.*
>
> *But in spring, he is Power itself.*

The Horned Lord is, in a word, magnificent. He is a living personification of the cycle of planting and harvest, winter and summer. But he also knows that he is but one personification of a principle that proceeds through the season, one face that the eternal Green Man wears.

In our own lives, we have multiple faces as well. The lesson the Horned Lord can teach us is to wear each face in its own time and to sometimes take off the masks entirely and be naked. At the Sacred Marriage of Beltane, the Horned Lord becomes naked, vulnerable, no longer alone—and at that moment the seeds of his birth, death, and birth again are planted.

Men wear masks. It's an occupational hazard, so to speak; we have to be different people at different times. Women wear masks as well, with one important difference. They haven't undergone the societal indoctrination that says that using one's mask to *keep others out* is part and parcel of being who they are. It took a very long time for me to allow other men to see me as I truly am—flawed yet powerful, shadowed yet incandescent, weak yet strong. Other men are supposed to be threats, and you never let a threat see you as you really are.

The Horned Lord is our talisman against that. *Be what you are when you need to be,* he says, *and all things are possible.*

The Horned Lord also has his darker side as well. He is the master of the Wild Hunt, the forces of Faerie who would hunt, catch, and kill mortals if they could. In this guise, he is unstoppable and implacable, a personification of the destruction inherent in nature and the wild, and of the fears that people have about them. The Master of the Hunt is the energy that dogs our steps in shadowed woods and on lonely roads. While our technological and urban society may have a skewed view of nature and its dangers, we can't escape the fact that there is a primal energy inherent in old, wild places that may be hostile—or at least uncaring. To portray that as caricature is dangerous. To ignore it is even more dangerous.

We've considered how powerful the horned figure is in mythology, appearing as it does in religious beliefs from Britain to India. It is in Greece, however, that this figure's most primal, frightening, and joyous manifestation ranges the hills of Arcadia.

The Boast of Pan

Know me, O man, and know I am Pan. I need no myth, no story, no tale. For I am a tale unto myself, every day writing another chapter in the long, delightful, and ribald jest that is my divine light.

I am the Horned One, who first arose in Arcadia. I am the shepherd of the gods. I am son to Zeus—or perhaps to Hermes. I shall not tell you; you shall guess for yourself. The Olympians may patronize me at times and view me as a country bumpkin cousin, but in their moments of honesty almost all will admit to having danced to my pipes, come to one of my parties, and reveled in my desires. If I am a country cousin, then truly do the country folk have more fun.

Homer said it best: I delight all the gods of Olympus. I gave Artemis her dogs and taught prophecy to Apollo. I play on the syrinx, and I give rise to dance and lust and delight—or, should it please me, I shall lay fear upon your heart in lonely dark places, for from thus comes the word "panic."

I am sex and lust and desire. I have pleased all the Maenads, and my name is whispered in their sweetest dreams. I am the unfettered spirit of masculinity, and my satyrs are like me in their desire for play and for love.

The Church tried to paint me as their Satan. I was feared, reviled, and called low and base. Plutarch claims I died; but if that were true it was my greatest jest, for I live again. I am invoked by modern Pagans more than I ever was in Greece.

Three words summarize the whole thing: Pan is desire. He's not the emotional side of the Lover; you aren't likely to see Pan writing a sonnet. Courtly love is definitely outside his bailiwick. He is musk and rut and desire—and there are few if any men who do not understand the energy behind him.

Let's face it: men are creatures of desire. We have the annoying tendency to have erections at impossible times, we are often slaves to our own penises, and we rarely think when desire hits us—all of which leads to paternity suits, presidential impeachments, and costly divorces. There isn't a man alive who doesn't understand that part of Pan, at least occasionally. Our only escape from it is exploring the myriad career options available for the twenty-first century eunuch.

My judgment is that men are usually afraid of that blinding tide of desire. We compensate for it by ignoring it, stuffing it and denying it exists, or by letting it turn us into whuffling pigs rooting for truffles of sexuality. (I've always liked that particular metaphor. I find it hilarious when the great philosopher Joe Bob Briggs calls sexual intercourse "aardvarking.")

So a lot of what institutional misandry, the hatred of men, says is true *is* true. Men are very much creatures of their desires. The point with which I personally differ is this: properly harnessed, this is a strength and not a weakness.

We know what desire feels like. That's a powerful, powerful thing; we know what it's like to really feel, really want something. It's what makes us restless, exploratory, and unwilling to settle for less; it's what makes us willing to step forth into the old, dark, wild landscape of body, mind, and soul to explore the shadows. That Pannic energy that all men have is what makes explorers, artists, inventors, creators, and fringe figures of all stripes refuse to settle for the status quo. And when a man falls into the bland world where he's settled for everything in his life, where there's nothing he truly wants, something dies—or worse, it breaks out in a moment of sheer anger, desire, and foolishness that destroys lives.

Yet Pan has a dark side, too. In the Greek myths, he's always off trying to assault some nymph. This doesn't make him that unusual—half the origin myths in Hellenic mythology involve a nymph changing into something to protect her virtue, but in Pan's case it's a very primal urge, the same urge that many of us men have felt. He is also the lord of fear, of "panic," who stalks dark places and whose pipes chill the very soul. He occasionally *likes* to scare people; that's part of who he is. If you think about it for a moment, that's part of what men are like, too; we get a rush sometimes by causing fear in others.

So how do we rise above it? By keeping our life in balance. My friend, ManKind Project brother, and covenmate Cernowain Greenman pointed out something brilliant to me about Pan: "I think where Pan strikes a balance between his desire and his intellect was when he played the pipes. Their sound is soft and soothing but laced with energetic desire that is somehow put under control. From his intellect comes the technique of releasing just the right amount of breath into just the right pipe to produce the notes of the tune."

As Pan balances and controls his breath, so too we need to balance our desires, our baser natures (you know, the ones that makes us look at someone and go, "I want to get me some of that NOW"), and our higher, creative, male selves. Pan taught prophecy and gave hounds to a goddess who in the standard interpretations of Olympian myth was not interested in men at all. Pan has always had his other side as keeper of the mysteries of the woods and mountains to balance off his day job as the host of *Maenads Gone Wild*. To deny that desire—that earthy, primal, sweaty, rutty inner self—is disaster. To indulge it without control is also disaster. It is only in the middle ground that we are fully male and still not slaves, able to participate in the cycle of our lives without getting carried away.

The Tale of the Death of Osiris

Osiris, whose name is also Asar, was the great king of the Egyptian people who taught them many arts. Eventually, he left to enlighten other lands, leaving his sister and his wife Isis as his regent.

While Osiris was gone, his brother Set attempted to seize the throne, murdering Osiris upon his return. The body of Osiris was put in a coffin and thrown into the Nile. Isis found the body, but Set tore it into fourteen pieces and scattered them throughout Egypt. Isis, with her magick, found the pieces, resurrected Osiris long enough to be impregnated by him, and bore Horus, who would reclaim the throne from Set.

Meanwhile, Osiris became the Lord and Judge of the Afterlife, admitting the dead to Duat, the fertile green world of the dead, providing that they passed his judgment. His eternal struggle with Set, god of the storms and the destructive power of the desert, reflected the precarious yet bountiful dependence on the Nile. As the flood waters receded every year, honors were paid to the Green Lord whose death means the crops will come again.

Let me state this for the record: I love Osiris. I have a personal relationship with him, as I do with Thoth, Set, and Bes, and my personal brand of eclectic Wicca has a strong Greco-Egyptian spin to its English roots.

Osiris is an incredibly potent example of the Green Man taken to its ultimate majestic conclusion: King, protector of the dead, lord of fertility, great sacrifice. Osiris is so many things wrapped up into one that he evokes awe in me—and awestruck worship is not something you see a lot in Pagans. (Incidentally, that's something I think is a bloody shame. The transcendent, transformative emotion of power and majesty is a baby that we threw out with the bathwater, and I'm climbing out the window to get the little sprout back.)

Osiris shows us another cycle of balance—the cycle between life and death, growth and decay. He addresses our fear of death directly, showing us that we will continue our individual journey as long as we carry ourselves with integrity, accountability, and honor. In Egyptian myth, Osiris was the judge of the dead; when a man died, he was brought by Anubis to the scale of Ma'at, where his heart was weighed against a feather. If it was lighter than the feather, he gained entrance to Duat; if it was heavier, it was consumed by the serpent Apep. Like Ellen Cannon Reed, I believe that Apep's devouring is not destruction but rather the return of the soul to the wheel of incarnations, moving on to another life to learn more.

In the ManKind Project, we are taught to create personal missions, statements of our life's goals and desires that we use as touchstones for self-assessment. Osiris is, to me, the Judge that my mission answers to. When I'm evaluated and weighed—for that matter, when I evaluate myself—I don't want anyone being "nice" to me. I want a good, hard edge; I want the truth. And in the death and rebirth of Osiris we have that edge. What judge would spare your feelings after he has returned from death? Alternately, why would he need to be cruel? The truth will suffice, and as men we need that kind of truth. In the cycle of creation and destruction Osiris represents, we can find that truth and we can find our missions and our purposes in life, so that we become that much closer to hearing Osiris say, "Enter to Duat, faithful man!"

Ellen Cannon Reed said it so well that I merely quote:

> As God of Vegetation, Asar would, of course, represent the life, death, and rebirth cycles of the grain and other plant life. Asar, Judge, Lord of Death, is concerned with the dead . . . the important thing to remember is that the Lord of Death is still the Lord of Life, one who has experienced death and rebirth.[25]

For Further Thought

Am I aware of when I wear my masks?

Am I in touch with both my higher and lower natures? And are they in balance?

Am I open to being judged?

<hr>

MAGICKAL WORKING

Growing Your Power

Got a green thumb? Considering painting your thumb green and hoping that's good enough? Have a thumb that isn't green, but you're willing to work at it? Then this working is for you. We're going to take a brief foray into the field of herbalism.

(Get it? Field. I slay myself sometimes.)

Let me make one thing perfectly clear: I am not an herbalist, in any way, shape, or form. I can grow herbs

---

25. Ellen Cannon Reed, *Circle of Isis* (Franklin Lakes, NJ: New Page Books, 2002), 34–37.

in pots and not screw it up about half the time. I cannot gather herbs in the wild, and I don't know what herbs are safe to take internally unless they show up in one of my cookbooks. I can't make tinctures, and my infusions are limited to Darjeeling.

However, a growing plant is a powerful magickal working in its own part. Sometimes the best symbol for the thing is the thing itself, and if you're looking to *grow* something, well, then, perhaps you should grow something.

If you have more interest in herbs past my kitchen gardening here, I encourage you to find reliable books on the matter, or better yet find a practicing herbalist to learn from.

Recommended Tools

- A good book or website on growing potted plants
- A small flowerpot, a trowel, and potting soil
- Herb cuttings or seeds
- A green candle

Light your smudge and call the directions (page 262).

Open the bag of potting soil. As you scoop—or even better, use your hands to move—the soil into the pot, say the following:

> *Great Green Lord, growing one, lord of death and birth,*
> *Let this soil nourish my desires as it nourishes a small piece of you.*
> *Let me feel the dirt in my hands, remembering my own nature as a child of the primal Earth.*
> *Let this be blessed.*

Now, plant your seed. I recommend finding a good gardening book or website and following the instructions for your individual choice of herb. Here are some possibilities:

- Basil—for love
- Borage—for courage
- Chamomile—for money
- Clover—for protection
- Sage—for cleansing
- Catnip—for happiness
- Mint—to develop psychic powers
- Carnation—for strength

Water your symbol of growth. Take care of it. Sometime between the waxing crescent and full moon every month, say the following over your herb:

> As this grows, so grows my desire.
> As this grows, so grows my will.
> Let this visible growth evoke growth in my life.
> Green Man, let this be blessed.

Do this for six lunar cycles. After that, harvest the plant and use it in some fashion—either by eating it[26] (nothing like spellwork that also helps furnish you with a dynamite Salad Caprese), or by drying it and adding it to your smudge.

---

26. Note: Do not eat any plant that is not meant to be eaten. Eating carnations is apparently possible, but I wouldn't recommend it on general principles.

Ritual of Affirmation

Acceptance of Fatherhood

This one's a biggie, folks.

I frankly have a real problem with the way we're treating fatherhood these days, and the blame is big enough to spread around. We're just past the dark ages when fathers were routinely denied custody of their children just for being male—in fact, there are still several organizations (including the National Fathers' Resource Center and the Single and Custodial Fathers' Network) that are dedicated to protecting the rights of fathers.

Here are the hard facts: Almost three and a half million children in the United States lived with a single father in 2006. Single-father families made up about 5 percent of all parent-child families that year.[27] Lots of guys out there are going it alone, more now than ever, but it's rare that you hear about it. Somehow, single dads aren't as heartwarming a human-interest story as other forms of families.

The word *father* is definitely off the A-list. I used to work in an office where single women referred to their "baby daddy." I *despise* that term, almost as much as I am desperately sad for the men who have so little presence in their children's lives that they become "baby daddies." I am a *father*. A "baby daddy" is a turkey baster or a Petri dish.

That said, there are many different ways one can be a father. The following rite is for a father who has fathered a child

---

27. U. S. Census Bureau, "America's Families and Living Arrangements: 2006. Table C2," www.census.gov/population/www/socdemo/hh-fam/cps2006.html (accessed September 12, 2007).

of his blood, an adoptive father, someone who has accepted the mantle of being someone else's surrogate father, a new step-father, or any one of a number of permutations. Family isn't those you're born into; it's who you choose to call family.

This ceremony is facilitated by the King, who should be a man who considers himself a father. The other archetypes should also be present to aid in facilitation. The tone for this is alternately solemn yet joyous and a little humorous; parenthood in and of itself holds all those energies. A simple altar should be laid with a God and Goddess candle, quarter candles, and symbols of the elements: a wand, a blade, a cup, and a stone. Any man in the circle who also claims fatherhood should carry a picture or other sign or symbol of his child or children.

The candidate enters the circle clad simply as he chooses. He should carry a small, blank book of the type used for journaling or Books of Shadows.

King: We welcome you to the circle of men. We also welcome you to the company of those who are fathers, whether fathers of the blood or fathers of the spirit. We are not merely the initiators of a biological process; we are men who have chosen to take full responsibility for what and whom we have created, or have accepted to guide and guard.

Youth: You have taken on a sacred charge: to provide wisdom, courage, humor, and above all, patience.

Warrior: You have taken on a sacred charge: you will guard your child with your life if need be.

Elder: You have taken on the most sacred charge of all: to teach others to be accountable, in integrity, and to grow into maturity. I salute you for accepting your responsibilities as a man does.

Youth: I call to the East, the spirits of Air! At dawn, the child awakes and reaches for his[28] father, who shows the child the rising sun. Hail and welcome, spirits of the East, essence of Air!

Warrior: I call to the South, the spirits of Fire! As the sun rises to its highest point, the father protects his child from the noonday heat while still allowing growth. Hail and welcome, spirits of the South, essence of Fire!

King: I call to the West, the spirits of Water! As the sun sets, the father supports the child on his first steps into the world. Hail and welcome, spirits of the West, essence of Water!

Elder: I call to the North, the spirits of Earth! In the darkest hour, the father becomes the Elder and his child in turn begins his own journey through parenthood. Hail and welcome, spirits of the North, essence of Earth!

Youth: We welcome the Great Goddess, Maiden, Mother, Crone, She who governs and guards the cycle of child to man to child again. Without the one, there cannot be the other. Hail, Great Goddess!

Elder: We welcome the Great God, king, warrior, magician, lover, He who is our model for divine

---

28. Change the pronoun genders throughout this ritual as appropriate.

masculinity. Without the one, there cannot be the other. Hail, Great God!

The men in the circle step forward, holding the tokens of their fatherhood.

Warrior: In the company of these assembled men, we ask you if you are ready to take on the burdens and the joys of fatherhood. You will need to be patient. You will need to be honest. You will need to be gentle. Do you swear that you will be in all things the best you can be, never letting anger dictate your actions?

Candidate acknowledges.

Youth: In the company of these assembled men, we ask you if you are ready to be childlike in your fatherhood. Are you willing to express joy, love, compassion? Are you willing to play, to believe, to seek? Are you willing to tell your child how magnificent he is and how much you love him?

Candidate acknowledges.

King: In the company of these assembled men, we ask you if you are ready to be just. Fatherhood sometimes requires you to be just without being merciful, to let a child suffer the consequences of his actions. Are you willing to let your child fall if his actions dictate it will be so, and to not shelter him from his own choices?

Candidate acknowledges.

Elder: Then state the name of your child and swear your willingness to take on that responsibility.

Candidate does so. This takes whatever form the candidate wishes: he can speak, sing, dance, do whatever he likes. The oath is serious; the content does not have to be.

King: Then, [*name*], we witness your self-declaration as father. May you find what you seek.

Elder: As an Elder of our tribe, I commend to you the watchword of the Green Man: *cycle*. Know that as you were a child, so too are you a father; as you are a father, so too will your child be a parent in time. This is the way: that we learn joy, so too shall we teach joy, and there shall be more light in the world. (*lays hand on forehead*) I bless you in the name of the Elder.

King: (*to the directions as he speaks*) The Earth of determination, the Water of love, the Fire of the spirit, and the Air of wisdom; we thank and bless their spirits, knowing they are with us always. May they guide you on your quest.

Youth: We thank the Great Goddess, She who is our other soul, for standing with us tonight.

Elder: We thank the Great God, He who is our root and our spirit, for standing with us tonight.

Warrior: Go now and begin your journey. We are with you always; come to us should you need our wisdom. We are your brothers.

VIII

THE GUIDE

IT'S NOT THE DESTINATION, IT'S THE ROAD

Someday historians will write about America in the twentieth century, and they'll say, "It was this weird time where people spent the first fifty years of their lives trying to figure out what they wanted to do, and the last twenty years regretting the fact they didn't start sooner."

—Joe Bob Briggs

It was only appropriate that I quote the immortal philosopher Joe Bob Briggs at the beginning of this chapter, because in this society our primary source for examples of the Guide is—yep, you guessed it—movies.

And we aren't talking about what Briggs, the Sage of Grapevine, would call "indoor bullstuff" movies either. We're talking *Star Wars*. *Lord of the Rings*. *The Karate Kid*. *Hoosiers*. Heck, you can even turn on the TV and see the Guide, albeit a bit unrecognizable and a touch quirky, in shows like *Hell's Kitchen* and *CSI*.

The Guide can also be called the Teacher, but there's an undercurrent to that that's not always appropriate. In mythological terms, the Guide will teach you what you want to know, but it will cost you; sometimes it even costs you your life, or at least the life you know. Teachers often have to be gentle; Guides are gentle or rough as the situation calls for. Teachers pass on knowledge; Guides may pass on knowledge, but they also pass on certain ineffable qualities that are not able to be explained, merely experienced. Guides don't just teach; they also inspire—and they're often likely to hand you a sandwich and a bad map and tell you to go find the lesson yourself.

In modern society, there are many Guide archetypes that affect how men act and how they are programmed. Teachers, drill instructors, police, coaches—all are reflections of the Guide, and they achieve their purpose with varying tactics. Everyone knows about the archetype of the brutal military officer or the coach who espouses "win at any cost," and to be fair, sometimes those reflect the truth of the situation. I would venture to say, though, that just as many men encounter supportive coaches and wise authority figures.

So why do we encounter so many distorted views of instructive authority? Let's face it: the dysfunctional guide makes better story. He's an easily portrayed, one-dimensional figure who makes a clear-cut villain, the literary equivalent of Spam—quick, easy, but not necessarily either good for you or real. Earlier in this work, we talked about the patriarchy victimizing men just as it victimizes women. This twisting of the Guide archetype is a perfect example; we've been programmed to *assume* that any authority figure who provides guidance is going to be vicious and without compassion, just as we've been programmed to assume that any hierarchy or authoritative structure is inherently corrupt. Because of that, as men we've almost completely lost touch with the Guide as an effective reality in our lives.

There is also a deeper reality we must admit to, though. As Jimmy N., one of my ManKind Project mentors, has said repeatedly: "Men are dangerous." We can't deny that. Men *are* dangerous; even in our most fully functional nature, we are in general willing to make failing at a lesson we teach have consequences. When it comes down to some fields, those consequences can include death. If we must fight, we need to be able to trust the man at our back to be capable of doing his job too. If he can't, he needs not to be there so as not to risk us as well.

The Guide is the refiner's fire, the crucible, what alchemists call the *athanor*. If we cannot pass through his fire, it is best to know that before we harm another.

The Tale of Hermes

Hermes is the child of Zeus and Maia, the Hellenic god of commerce, invention, cunning, and theft. Yet like most of the Greek deities, he has other faces. The Guide can be seen in two of them, Hermes Enodios and Hermes Psychopompos.

Hermes Enodios is the guardian of roads, crossroads, and travel. He is, literally, the Guide; before a journey is undertaken, prayers are offered to him for safe passage. He embodies crossing a boundary, be it a physical boundary such as a crossroads or a more spiritual boundary such as a life change, a transcendent or transitional activity, or any moment when a man moves from one state to other. As Hermes Psychopompos, he becomes the escort for the dead, escorting souls into—and, rarely, out of—Hades.

Whenever souls move, there is Hermes. He brings dreams to mortals. In one version of Pandora's tale, he was the source for both Pandora's fatal curiosity and her rediscovery of the hope remaining in the bottom of her box. He escorted Kore—Persephone—back into the upper world and restored her to the care of her mother, Demeter. He led Orpheus into Hades to beg for the life of

> his beloved Eurydice—and when Orpheus failed to meet
> Hades' terms and Eurydice was doomed to death, Hermes
> led her back to the kingdom of Hades.
>
> As Hermes Enagonios, he was the patron of athletic
> games, and those games were—are—about transcending
> boundaries. That sense of the Guide's role is reflected in
> the modern Olympic motto—Citius, Altius, Fortius—
> "swifter, higher, stronger."
>
> Hermes leads us to our boundaries and leaves us to
> pass them or not as our own strength sees fit.

That is a whole lot of work for one god, or so it seems. But
Hermes is the Gatekeeper, the warden of transfer, the Guide
who leads us from one state to another. Men spend their entire
lives moving from one state to another; our life is mapped out
in milestones—and milestones belong to Hermes.

Hermes teaches us not to be in a hurry. Take time to
smell the roses—or, better yet, hang out and enjoy the
moment. He's relaxed, he's easy—but when our time comes
to die, it may be Hermes who escorts us to wherever it is we
will go. And Hermes will go anywhere; it's not a mistake
that he's also the patron of thieves, gamblers, and other low
members of society. Hermes will take us wherever we need
to go, but our safety and our ability to learn and get to our
destination is our problem. There are no seat belts, there are
no money back guarantees, and you may not end up where
your carefully laid plans think you should be.

That's a heavy dichotomy, but in it we see one simple
truth: that every moment is a new moment, and every
change has the capability of being life-changing. Yet, if we

hold on to where we are—if we refuse to move on—then we fossilize and stop growing. The human spirit is like a shark; it must move to feed and feed to live. But sometimes men have to pay a heavy price for wisdom.

The Tale of Mimir and Odin

In the beginning when the giants and primal gods ruled the worlds, Mimir was the source of all knowledge and wisdom. He guarded the well from which one drink would grant knowledge of the past, present, and future, and he kept his counsel to himself.

In those days, Odin and his brothers Vili and Ve had slain the giant Ymir and of his flesh made the earth, Midgard, the place of mortals. And then did Odin create man and woman—but he still desired greater wisdom. So he put on the shape of a wanderer and came to Mimir bargaining for a drink of his well.

Mimir named a price and Odin paid it. Odin's left eye was left in the fountain, and Odin was granted his drink. At that moment Odin saw past, present, and future, and saw the sorrows and troubles that would plague god and man and what Odin could do to assuage them somewhat. So, in the words of the Hávamál, Odin sacrificed himself:

137. I trow I hung on that windy Tree
nine whole days and nights,
stabbed with a spear, offered to Odin,
myself to mine own self given,
high on that Tree of which none hath heard
from what roots it rises to heaven.

138. None refreshed me ever with food or drink,

> *I peered right down in the deep;*
> *crying aloud I lifted the Runes*
> *then back I fell from thence.*[29]

Nine nights did Odin hang on the tree, alone, and returned with the runes—a legacy of Mimir's granting of wisdom at a price.

In time, Mimir was slain and beheaded—some say by the Vanir, some say by another. Yet Odin was so wise that he was able to keep Mimir's head alive and turned to it often for counsel.

Mimir is the teacher. Odin is the student. Yet in the end, the student becomes the adept, and the teacher moves to advise him, taking a background role to the student's magnificence. This is in many ways a natural and archetypical cycle, yet it's a cycle that can be sidetracked by ego. Think how many plays, movies, books, and television shows have as their central plot point the young prodigy and the old master, and the conflict between them—the conflict in which the old refuses to be supplanted by the new because of ego or insecurity.

There's a central bit of wisdom to that; in order for a man to successfully evoke the Guide within him, he must be willing to put the ego aside and not be the central figure in the tale any longer. It's not Obi-Wan who defeats Darth Vader; it's Luke, long after Obi-Wan has given his life to buy time for the young rebels. Frodo, not Gandalf, destroys Sauron. This state of "stepping aside" can even be seen in one

---

29. *The Elder or Poetic Edda*, trans. by Olive Bray (London: The Viking Society, 1908).

of my favorite TV shows, *Queer Eye*: five Guides come in, provide wisdom for a man (and in my opinion, the guidance they provide is essential and sadly overlooked; a man used to know how to groom himself properly and how to entertain), and then absent themselves from the final big occasion where the newly-made man is unveiled.

That stepping aside is essential to the Guide's inner nature. That's why divine Guides rarely play center stage in their myths; it's not their nature to do so.

The Tale of Merlin

Merlin was the child of a Welsh princess, born out of wedlock; some say his father was an angel or an incubus, but others say he was a lord of Faerie. No matter what the genealogy, Merlin was a child with many strange powers.

Vortigern, one of the claimants to the throne after the Roman withdrawal from Britain, had come to Dinas Emrys in Wales to try to make a stand and build a great fortress. The building kept falling, and Vortigern was told that the building required the sacrifice of a fatherless child; Merlin, of course, was brought to him. Merlin advised him of the truth of the matter—that two dragons, one red and one white, one representing the Saxons and one the Bretons, fought underground, below the keep. The red dragon eventually drove the white one back, and Merlin prophesied Vortigern would fall. This came to pass, and eventually Uther Pendragon came to the throne.

Merlin allowed Uther to seduce Igraine through his magick, and Igraine gave birth to Arthur. He became Arthur's tutor, and gained him the sword Excalibur and

*its even more powerful scabbard. Yet the same Lady of
the Lake who gave the sword trapped Merlin in a crystal cave and took him away from Arthur—so that in
Arthur's hour of need Merlin's wisdom was unavailable,
and Camelot fell. Merlin was tricked by the Lady, teaching her all his magick and falling in love with her, only to
be betrayed and imprisoned.*

I would just like to state that I have always considered Merlin's fate to be one of the most ridiculous things I have ever
read. You have this all-powerful, half-human, supernatural,
all-seeing, wise wizard of great repute being imprisoned
because he is suddenly thinking with the wrong head. I will
be the first one to admit that love—or lust—makes a man do
silly things. But this, my friends, is pushing it.

This has bugged me for years. (That either says something about how young I was when I first was exposed to the
Arthurian cycle—I had read Malory at least four years before
my father took me to see John Boorman's *Excalibur* in the
theatre when I was ten years old—or how weird I am.) Why
would Merlin be so thrice-damned *stupid*?

One day, out of the blue, a question surfaced from the
morass of my subconscious that I had to stop and really
think about:

What if Merlin *meant* to do it?

We've talked about how the Guide must, at some point,
remove himself from center stage, abandon his ego, and let
the hero take the story wherever it needs to go. Yet Merlin
had two great disadvantages: he could see the future and by
all accounts he loved Arthur as a son.

Under those circumstances, could you walk away—even though you knew you had to? I don't know if I could. The Arthurian myth cycle is, in its most common interpretation, a tragedy. Arthur dies, Lancelot dies, Gawain dies, *everybody* dies—and if you don't die, you get to be like Guinevere and spend the rest of your life angsting in a convent somewhere. This is not a happy story. And yet it's a story in which you can see how the tragedy takes place; the moment Lancelot trots on to the scene, his teeth shining like a Pepsodent commercial, perhaps with "C'est Moi" from *Camelot* playing in the background, you can see the fatal flaws in everybody involved.

There are some situations even a half-Sídhe grand wizard Guide can't fix.

How many times as men do we keep trying to fix a situation we know is hopeless? As men, we are programmed to believe that it's our job to stay on duty no matter what, saluting bravely as the ship sinks around us instead of looking for a life preserver and getting the hell off the ship. We get ourselves in situations where self-preservation—emotional, physical, and spiritual—tells us to get out, and yet we stay. We stay because we're men, we're tough, and we're supposed to stay, darn it. We stay in loveless and sexless marriages, shit jobs, abusive habits, and dysfunctional families because we aren't allowed to feel, to be afraid, and to run for our ever-loving lives.

Merlin as Guide teaches us that that's a slow form of suicide. We must find the balance between our inner heroes and our sometimes-lacking source of self-preservation. Merlin may fool himself, not seeing what's coming—but I think it's more likely that the out given him by the Lady of the Lake lets him walk away from the train wreck that he cannot see a way to avoid.

For Further Thought

Am I taking time to smell the roses, to learn the lessons from my surroundings?

Am I able to put my ego aside to teach another?

Am I currently trying to save a situation that is hopeless?

MAGICKAL WORKING

Hearing the Inner Guide

All of us have a spirit guide. For our purposes, it's immaterial whether or not you view the guide as something external or something internal; it's a voice coming from somewhere other than your conscious mind that provides you with valuable information.

In order to hear that guide in this magickal working, we're going to use a technique called automatic writing.

Recommended Tools

- Writing implements. You can use a pen and paper, a computer and keyboard, or anything else you're comfortable transcribing data with.

- A purple candle.

- Relaxation music. Only use this if you're one of those people who relaxes well to music. If silence works better for you, then by all means be silent.

Light your smudge and call the directions (page 262).

Light the purple candle and look into its flame. Say the following:

Great Guide, lord of wisdom,
   I open myself to your voice in this place.
   Bless me with the answers to the questions in my heart.
   Let the voice I open myself bring knowledge without malice.

While thinking about the question you want to ask or the matter you want guidance on, carefully write or type that question on a blank screen or sheet of paper. Then close your eyes and relax. Let your entire body relax for a moment, then slip deeper into a trance-like state. (If you have some trouble with this, check the instructions for basic centering in appendix I.)

Once you have achieved a state of centered calm, begin typing or writing. Don't worry about what you're writing; just let the words flow from the guide within to the reality without. Don't backspace, question, correct, or cross out; even typos have meaning in this altered state. Relax and let it flow.

When you feel the message is complete, stop. Slowly bring yourself out of trance. Read what you've written. It may not make sense right now; that's okay. Extinguish the candle.

For nine nights after, light the candle and by its light consider the words the Guide has given you.

RITUAL OF AFFIRMATION

Becoming the Mentor

The need for this ritual may not seem evident at first. But let's consider the role of a mentor in our society for a moment.

In general, we have no organized programs of apprenticeship anymore. Information is rarely if ever passed down from a man to another man or to youths. We live in a world of training classes, self-guided website learning, and two-hundred-seat lecture halls. The personal touch is seriously lacking. So for a man to take on mentorship—be it teaching, coaching, being a magickal teacher or mentor, being a Big Brother, or any form of instruction—is a sacred charge, more so when such an activity is rarely if ever seen as sacred from a societal standpoint.

Once upon a time, men were named by the trade they followed. While I do not advocate going back to those times —usually, back then, a man was a farmer and gave almost all his harvest to some noble lord somewhere because that's all he *could* do—I do think that it's an energy that could be reclaimed in a modified fashion. A man's trade is not necessarily what he gets paid for; it's what makes him feel complete—his vocation, his purpose. As a sacred community of men, we should and we will honor this.

This ritual is facilitated by the Youth, Warrior, King, and Elder, along with a circle of men. The men in the circle may, if they like, carry or wear some token of their chosen trade. A simple altar should be laid with a God and Goddess candle, quarter candles, and symbols of the elements: a wand, a blade, a cup, and a stone.

The candidate enters the circle clad as he wills. He carries a token of the mentorship he is about to undertake. The King steps forward.

King: In order to have mysteries, we must have knowledge. In order to have knowledge, we must remember our past. In order to remember our past, we must make it a living tradition. In order to make it a living tradition, we must pass it on. In order to pass it on, we must become teachers.

Youth: In our tribe, the tribe of men, teachers are sacred. The role of a mentor is to shape and prepare another man or a youth to find his vocation and his purpose in life, to find the thing that makes his heart sing, the role that the God and the Goddess prepared for him in this incarnation.

King: In order to be teachers, we must know our craft. In order to know our craft, we must know ourselves. In order to know ourselves, we must know our light and our shadow.

Warrior: Being a mentor is difficult, sometimes thankless, usually exhausting. You must have patience, forbearance, balance. You must be willing to speak the language of another, to help him gain the wisdom you hold.

King: In order to know our light and our shadow, we must know our weaknesses. In order to know our weaknesses, we must know our strengths.

Elder: At this time, in the company of these assembled men, are you willing to accept the burden and the ecstasy of mentorship?

Candidate acknowledges.

King: In order to know our strengths, we must embrace our own sacredness.

Elder: State to these assembled men your intention for mentorship.

The candidate at this time describes his hopes, fears, and desires for his upcoming mentorship. *He may provide as little or as much information as he wants, but he should focus on the feelings he has, the fears he has, and the outcome he would like to see from the process.*

Youth: You have declared your intention to be called teacher. Do you swear to tell the truth to your students, to instruct them to the best of their abilities, and to provide a just and fair assessment and testing of their abilities?

Warrior: A mentor is an authority figure, often put on pedestals—and as such in our society may have temptations to take advantage of a student financially, emotionally, sexually, or spiritually. Do you swear to resist those temptations, to charge only what is fair and reasonable should such be appropriate, and to never abuse your position of authority for your own gratification?

King: Do you swear to uphold ethical standards for your students, teaching them that we behave in a sacred manner because we live in a sacred world, the importance of just and fair play, and the importance of finding their own trade and vocation?

Elder: Lastly, do you swear to, when the time comes, release your student from your instruction, when you have no more to teach?

Candidate so swears.

King: Then, [*name*], we witness your self-declaration as mentor. May you bring light to others' darkness.

Warrior: As a Warrior of our tribe, I commend to you the watchword of the Guide: *challenge.* Know that the role of the teacher is to, first and foremost, challenge the student—challenging preconceptions, challenging ignorance, challenging boundaries. There is room for caregiving as well, but at times the teacher must be the hard edge of the blade.

King: (*to the directions as he speaks*) The Earth of determination, the Water of love, the Fire of the spirit, and the Air of wisdom: we thank and bless their spirits, knowing they are with us always. May they guide you on your quest.

Youth: We thank the Great Goddess, She who is our other soul, for standing with us tonight.

Elder: We thank the Great God, He who is our root and our spirit, for standing with us tonight.

Warrior: Go now and begin your journey. We are with you always; come to us should you need our wisdom. We are your brothers.

IX

THE CRAFTSMAN
FORGING, SHAPING, TESTING, BECOMING

The moment we fully and vitally realize who and what we are, we then begin to build our own World even as God builds his.

—Ralph Waldo Trine

The next two divine faces in our examination of the gods and ourselves are in many ways mirrors of each other. The Craftsman and the Magician are both masters of arcane arts, knowledge that is limited and held in trust, special techniques that to the outsider may seem mysterious and incomprehensible. More importantly, to be either a Craftsman or a Magician is to become something, to change; no one is born with a facility in either. It is learned with time and practice. It is, at its heart, an extension of your will.

There is, however, a major dichotomy in how we *view* these two archetypes. The Craftsman, our focus in this chapter, is often seen as a simple laborer, a worker, someone who may or may not be in tune with the mysteries of the Universe. In truth, most people assume he's more in tune with the realities of his everyday life. People rarely think of plumbers as being great theoreticians in metaphysics.

My general thought is "more fool they." While it's true that the Magician's arts are primarily of the mind and the Craftsman's primarily of the hands, they share a great deal of common ground. The difference is that the Craftsman creates while the Magician changes—and even that's not a hard and

fast rule. The Craftsman is the yang to the Magician's yin—
yet most of the time we sell the Craftsman short mentally.

I have some personal investment in this. My father, Patrick, who died in 1991, was a Craftsman archetype through and through. I grew up in a pretty bad home environment, due to an alcoholic grandmother and a drug-using mother—and like my father, I was often caught in the middle. One of the few islands of peace I can remember is my father's downstairs workshop, where with an astonishingly light touch he built small houses and other buildings out of wood. Most of them ended up as crèches, and he gave many of them to friends and family. He was a pretty good scratch carpenter as well; he turned the third floor of our old house into two more bedrooms. Even now, there's not a day that goes by when I don't wish I could pick up the phone and call him.

So obviously the Craftsman is near and dear to my heart, and my first exposure to his mysteries was my father and his hot glue gun and his scraps of wood. And had anyone assumed my father was a shallow man, they would have been sadly mistaken. His parents couldn't afford to send him to college, so he worked all his life in manual labor; he was at various times a sandhog, a produce unloader, a retail manager, a small appliance repairman, and a warehouse foreman. He also read voraciously, owned a collection of science fiction to rival mine, and constantly watched public television. He could appreciate equally Jefferson Airplane and Beethoven. He was a huge fan of both baseball (I cried when the White Sox won the World Series in 2005, because I wished Dad could have seen it—now if only the Cubs could do the same) and drum corps. He was a great cook and a great father.

To me, when I think of the Craftsman, I think of my dad.

So what is the Craftsman, anyway? To me, he is the divine archetype of making, creating, becoming. He's different, though, from the Creator in that he seems to favor a more hands-on approach, and in most cases he is the direct patron of the manufacturing and building arts. He is often called upon to create objects of divine power, sometimes lent to favored mortals, and as such serves as a channel of power and majesty from the gods to men.

The Craftsman is about the details, about taking care of the very small things and making sure that every little bit is done properly with as much skill and care as possible. Even if it's a Universe.

The Tale of Ptah

Ptah was the first of the gods, the spirit of creation and life who envisioned the Universe. He created the gods first. Ptah imagined the gods in his heart: Atum, Shu, Tefnut, Geb, Nut, Osiris, Isis, Set, and Nephythys. He then spoke the words and the visions of his heart became reality. "Every word of the god came about through what the heart devised and the tongue commanded."[30]

Ptah's name means "opener" or "sculptor." He created the heavens and the earth while Khnum, the potter god, spun

---

30. From the creation myth the Memphite Theology, quoted at Marie Parsons, "Egypt: Egyptian Creation, A Feature Tour," www.touregypt.net/featurestories/creation.htm (accessed May 29, 2007).

> *the animals and people into being on his pottery wheel—all through the words of his Tongue and the thoughts of his Heart. When men die, Ptah is he who grants them life in the afterlife, or return to another life. He also grants the dead speech through the Opening of the Mouth ritual. He is the initiator, the speaker, the creator—the first of the gods of Egypt, and the one who knows many mysteries.*

There is one line in that tale that absolutely cuts to the heart of the matter: ". . . through the words of his Tongue and the thoughts of his Heart." That is the important part, right there: *what we desire and what we speak is what we get.* This is the central essence of magick, power, achievement—whatever you want to call changing yourself and the world. We get what we put into the world, and we therefore have a responsibility to put forth good into the world if we want good back. One of my favorite websites, that of the Ontario Consultants on Religious Tolerance, cites no less than twenty-one different religions espousing some variation on this principle, called the Ethics of Reciprocity or the Golden Rule.[31]

I think it needs to be taken even further, however. Various branches of Judaism have a principle known as *tikkun olam* that I cheerily admit I filed the serial numbers off of and stole for my own personal spirituality. (I do that.)

What *tikkun olam* means, literally, is "repairing the world." While there are many interpretations of the phrase, one interpretation states that for every act of justice and

---

31. "Shared Belief in the 'Golden Rule'" Ontario Consultants on Religious Tolerance, www.religioustolerance.org/reciproc.htm (accessed May 29, 2007).

goodness performed, the Universe becomes that much closer to perfection, to its original purpose. What we speak and what we do is truly what we get back; each act of light brings more light into the world, and each act of negativity keeps the world flawed, broken, dark. In some branches of Jewish thought, the process of returning the Universe to its initial perfection expresses the ability of humanity to share in the divine process of creation.

The important thing to keep in mind here is that part of the Craftsman's purpose is to repair the flawed, the broken, the lost. Each act performed with the true will of the Craftsman is *tikkun olam*, and in Ptah's tale we see the ultimate expression of that principle: that what we do with will affects the Universe. Ptah's lesson is that every small act changes the world—that, in fact, any act done with will may change the world in great, sweeping, unexpected ways.

The Tale of Hephaestus

Hephaestus was the son of Hera, conceived by her own will. He was brought to life to free Athena from Zeus, who had swallowed her mother whole to keep Athena from being born. Yet Hephaestus was weak, with a lame leg, and so Hera threw him out of heaven. He fell for nine days and nine nights and landed on the island of Lemnos, where he built his smithy.

In retaliation, Hephaestus built a great throne and sent it to heaven for Hera. She sat in it and it imprisoned her, and Hephaestus would not release her. Finally, Dionysus plied Hephaestus with wine, and he was brought to heaven. He only agreed to release Hera when Aphrodite was given to him as a bride.

Hephaestus and Aphrodite's marriage was not without its problems. When the Goddess of Love began having an affair with Ares, Hephaestus forged a chain net so strong that even a god could not break it and imprisoned Ares and Aphrodite while they were dallying. Hephaestus showed the scene to the assembled gods, who roared with laughter at the ridiculousness of it. Hephaestus then married Aglaea, one of the Graces.

Hephaestus manufactured many great gifts for the gods, including Zeus's thunderbolts, Eros's arrows, Athena's shield Aegis, and the sun chariot of the god Helios who piloted the sun across the sky.

It's really easy to read a great deal into Hephaestus. He has, as we say, issues.

But what I want to focus on is his lameness and his desire for retribution against those who reject him. Those things don't go hand in hand, but in his case they do seem to interrelate. A maimed god, he's first rejected by his mother—who gave birth to him by herself—and then cuckolded by the bride he earned after freeing his mother from the revenge he took on her for rejecting her. I'm not saying this is a convoluted situation, but I frankly suspect there are soap operas that would turn it down as being implausible.

Bill Kauth, in his brilliant book *A Circle of Men*, quotes psychologist James Hillman: "'Every man's life mission is rooted in his little boy's deepest need.'"[32] It's pretty obvious from this that a great deal of the deepest need of Hephaestus is rooted in being rejected and "cast from heaven." Remember that the Hellenic gods were viewed as being very human, and therefore had human motivations.

The real question becomes: why did Hephaestus *change*? The myths are silent on that, but I have my own theories. I think Hephaestus *willed* to move past it. There comes a point in life at which our myriad rejections and hurts that we've suffered become almost too much to continue to maintain. Every man, at some point, chooses whether or not to find the strength to decide if his past and his limitations are going to define him, if he will remain their prisoners. Richard Bach said: "Argue for your limitations, and sure enough, they're yours."[33] The lesson we learn from Hephaestus is that sometimes you can transcend those limitations, and more importantly sometimes it doesn't seem obvious from the outside as to why or how you can. Sometimes it's merely the extension of true will that gets us through the dark night of the soul and into the next morning—whatever that morning may be. In the case of Hephaestus, he settles down with Aglaea.

Most interesting is that after Hephaestus gets past his early days of drama among the Olympians, he's not heard from much anymore. He's stable, useful, and settles down to what is apparently an ordinary life of thunderbolt fashioning.

---

32. Bill Kauth, *A Circle of Men: The Original Manual for Men's Support Groups* (New York: St. Martin's, 1992), 81.

33. Richard Bach, *Illusions: The Adventures of a Reluctant Messiah* (New York: Delacorte Press, 1977), 75.

It's like the Olympian equivalent of *Leave It to Beaver*: "How was it at the smithy today, honey?" "Oh, fine, fine, made a bunch of thunderbolts and worked on the transmission of that sun chariot. Sticky bit of work."

Hephaestus is the spirit and patron of every man who willed that enough was enough and refused to be drawn into the dramas of his dysfunctions. He is also the patron of every man who continues his Great Work while overcoming a physical limitation; I've never understood why more disabled Pagans aren't drawn to the worship of Hephaestus. In the fire of his forge, we can choose to just walk away from the rejections others lay on us.

The difficulty, though, comes when we have laid rejections, preconceptions, or limitations on ourselves. Those can often suffocate us more than outside influences—and they're harder to shed.

The Tale of Ilmarinen

Seppo Ilmarinen, the Eternal Hammerer, is the blacksmith and inventor of the Kalevala, the great Finnish mythic cycle. When his brother Väinämöinen, the great sage and magician, was captured by the queen of Pohjola, the land of the north, Ilmarinen offered his services to free him. The great queen, Louhi, a powerful wizard in her own right, demanded that Ilmarinen make the Sampo, a powerful artifact, and she would not only free Väinämöinen, she would give him her daughter for Ilmarinen's wife.

Ilmarinen worked night and day, and the Sampo took many forms—but all the forms were flawed, somehow destructive or bloodthirsty. Finally, Ilmarinen begged the

*four winds to fan the flames of his forge, and the Sampo
was created. Louhi freed Väinämöinen—but her daughter
refused to marry Ilmarinen.*

*Ilmarinen in his sorrow tried to forge himself a wife.
He created a woman out of silver and gold, but she was
hard and cold and did not make him happy. Saddened, he
tries to offer the wife to Väinämöinen, who rejects her in
one of the Kalevala's most famous stanzas:*

> *Every child of Northland, listen,*
> *Whether poor, or fortune-favored:*
> *Never bow before an image*
> *Born of molten gold and silver:*
> *Never while the sunlight brightens,*
> *Never while the moonlight glimmers,*
> *Choose a maiden of the metals,*
> *Choose a bride from gold created*
> *Cold the lips of golden maiden,*
> *Silver breathes the breath of sorrow.*[34]

The tale of Ilmarinen is usually viewed as a cautionary tale
about the pursuit of gold and why it is damaging to the
soul. That's a useful assessment, but for our purposes I think
there's another lesson to be learned here.

How many men seek to find all the answers in their
work? Everything can be solved if you just work hard enough,
wear your nose away at the proverbial grindstone, bust your

---

34. *The Kalavela.* Compiled by Elias Lönnrot. Translated by John Martin Crawford
(1888). From the Internet Sacred Text Archive, www.sacred-texts.com/neu/
kveng/index.htm (accessed May 29, 2007).

ass. Work harder, work faster, work more, and lose yourself in your work, and everything will make sense.

Wow, that's a rough thought. "Lose yourself in your work." Because there are many men who are lost in their work and think that it contains all the answers. Now I cheerfully admit that I have rarely if ever held a "real" job. (Let's look at the list: drive-time DJ, magazine editor who worked from home, sommelier, waiter, freelance writer, cattery assistant (yes, I really was one summer), night-shift operator for a dispatching service, weekend fill-in DJ . . . nope. Very few "real" jobs.) I was a stay-at-home father for years. But I have known many guys who lost themselves in their work. It's actually really tragic, because there's so much more life to be lived that they're missing.

Suppose Ilmarinen would have found himself a girlfriend if he'd actually *left* the smithy once in a while? Suppose he really desired what he was looking for? Or when it came right down to it, was the search more of a personal drama than the finding? One interpretation of this story is that Ilmarinen's metal wife was unsatisfactory because of sexual shortcomings. Let's face it: skin and a warm body are rather a requirement for sexual happiness, but they're rarely mapped territory for the Craftsman in his purest form.

The cautionary note here is to realize that the Craftsman is just one archetype of many, and to embrace it too far results in a life that is fundamentally unsatisfying. Ilmarinen is—and remains—lonely because he can't redefine himself as something more than a smith. Now he may be the best and baddest smith in the entire *Kalevala*, but that doesn't keep him company at night. He's unable to step outside the boundaries he's defined for himself; he's unable, to use a cli-chéd phrase, to "think outside the box." He can't come up with a solution for his loneliness other than to bargain his smithing skills or try to smith himself up the most high-functioning blow-up doll in existence. He's unable to will himself into a new self-definition.

For Further Thought

Am I repairing or destroying the world?

Am I still in thrall to my anger, or have I transcended it?

Are my self-definitions limiting how I approach the places in my life that I want to improve?

MAGICKAL WORKING

Forgiving the Wound

I had a lot of trouble coming up with a magickal working for the Craftsman chapter. Frankly, the best one has already been done: Bill Kauth's "Discovering Your Mission" from *A Circle of Men* is a hugely valuable tool in men's work and in this particular archetypical work.

Yet as I thought about it, I thought about wounds. Quite often, what we want in life—what we want the Craftsman archetype to help us fashion—is something we didn't have as a child. That lack, that absence, that wound can mean we lash out through destructive behavior, either at ourselves or at others. When the time comes that we turn to channeling our energies toward healing and move towards being fully functional men, a time may come when we need to forgive others or ourselves for what has been done. That's where this working comes in.

Recommended Tools

- A small cloth bag of some color that signifies healing to you. Blue is the traditional color, and it works well.

- A piece of glass or a broken crystal. Make sure it has no sharp or dangerous edges—safety first.

- Enough salt to fill the bag about three-quarters full.

- A blue candle.

Light your smudge and call the directions (page 262).

Light the candle and hold the crystal in your right hand. Meditate for a moment on the wrong you want to forgive yourself for, or the past wound you want to move beyond. Say the following:

> *Great Craftsman whose will creates rather than destroys,*
>> *Give me the strength and the fire of your forge*
>> *To move past my own past, the wrongs I have done*
>> *and the wrongs done to me.*
>> *Let me be more than the sum of my experiences.*
>> *Let me begin anew here, tempered in the crucible of my will.*
>> *Let this wound be healed.*

Lay your hand on the sand.

> *As sand is reforged to be glass,*
>> *As stone is reforged to be crystal,*
>> *So do I consecrate this sand to be the instrument of my*
>> *reforging.*
>> *Let it be so.*

Fill the bag halfway full with sand, and then place the glass or crystal inside the bag. Finish filling the bag with sand, full enough that the glass or crystal remains held within the sand.

This wound will not go away; it is a part of me.
Yet my reaction to it can change.
I can forgive; I can be renewed, reforged so that it no longer shapes me
But I shape it.

Tie the bag shut with three knots.

Great Craftsman, consecrate this work and let me move forward with my life.

The bag can be thrown into running water or buried in a dark place.

RITUAL OF AFFIRMATION

Blessing of a Place of Work

This strikes me as a good time to talk about smudge.

For as long as humanity has had ceremonies, someone has decided that those ceremonies needed to involve burning something. Be it wood, leaf, stem, or flower, various ignited aromatics have been involved with rituals for a very long time.

Now, I like smudge. I also like incense. Given my druthers, I'd be burning incense whenever I decided it would be cool to do so—which would be very often. However, I've also lived with an asthmatic.

So use smudge/incense as you want, or don't use it. You'll notice the magickal workings in this book call for it; you can also cheerfully ignore that.

If you do use smudge, I'm going to challenge you to step outside the usual white sage. While that's a valid smudging technique, it's also specifically from one spiritual tradition (Native American). Most of us are not First Nations; it would be an honor to our own heritages, whatever they are, to find something from our own tribe. (I also have issues about Caucasians co-opting Native American traditions, but that's my shame issue.) I like lavender and bay myself, with just a touch of sage. Chamomile is nice. In short, think outside the box magickally. That said . . .

This is a ritual to bless a man's new undertaking—a new business, a new place of work, some material space that exemplifies him moving forward on his Hero's Journey. With a little adjustment, it could even be used as a house blessing. This is a portable ceremony, so to speak, designed to move throughout a place of business if it has multiple rooms. As such, there are only a few tools used:

The Youth carries an incense or smudge burner.

The Warrior carries a sword or ritual knife.

The King carries a coin or some other representation of wealth—a silver dollar works really well, especially if you can find an old one that's actually made of silver.

The Elder carries some sort of magickal tool—it can be a wand, a staff, whatever the Elder is comfortable with. For elemental symmetry, it should have or contain a stone or crystal.

If possible, the assembled participants gather outside the door to the place of business. Each one should carry a small, inexpensive object to contribute to a ritual bag to celebrate the blessing.

The Youth lights the smudge as the Elder speaks.

Elder: We are gathered here to bless a man in a new undertaking. This is a dream this man has crafted— a new venue for his dreams, his creative strength. As you step through the smudge and bless yourself, keep in your thoughts the risk this man is taking and the blessings you bring him on this day.

Each man blesses himself with the smudge as he enters.

Youth: (*blessing the space with smudge or incense*) May this place be blessed with Air. May there be wisdom, knowledge, and skill; may those who come here find what they seek.

Warrior: (*blessing the space with knife or sword*) May this place be blessed with Fire. May there be passion and caring here; may those who come here be helped and be honored as customers and as friends.

King: (*blessing the space with coin*) May this place be blessed with Water. May there be bounty and harvest here; may those who work here find riches material and spiritual while still being in integrity with themselves and others.

Elder: (*blessing the space with wand*) May this place be blessed with Earth. May there be grounding and sustenance here; may this place and those within it be safe from harm and may they grow and flourish.

At this time, if necessary or desired, additional rooms are blessed in the same or similar format. Once that is done, the participants gather back in the main room of the establishment.

The owner(s) of the establishment step forward.

Warrior: Any dream requires investment—investment of time, talent, material, money, heart, soul. We bless you for taking this risk, for asking yourself, "Why not?"

Elder: And your friends around you bless you as well. They have brought small symbols or tokens of their desire to have your dream take flight. At this time, they will gift you with their hopes for you.

The assembled participants present their gifts to the owner(s), explaining briefly what each object symbolizes as they are so moved to do. As each one is given, the previous one is taken by the Youth and placed in a small sacred bag. Once that process is finished:

King: This assembled sacred bundle is a symbol of your friends' and colleagues' good wishes for your new undertaking. Let it be a blessing to you and a reminder that many people stand behind you in your work.

Elder: As an Elder of our tribe, I commend to you the watchword of the Craftsman: *will.* Know your will in what you build here; know what it is you want, and keep your desires in front of you and your fears in front of you as you go forth.

King: *(to the directions as he speaks)* The Earth of determination, the Water of love, the Fire of the spirit, and the Air of wisdom: we thank and bless their spirits, knowing they are with us always. May they guide you on your quest.

Youth: We thank the Great Goddess, She who is our other soul, for standing with us tonight.

Elder: We thank the Great God, He who is our root and our spirit, for standing with us tonight.

Warrior: Go now and begin your journey. We are with you always; come to us should you need our wisdom.

Place the sacred bag somewhere within the establishment, hung over a door or under the counter, to bring in prosperity.

X

THE MAGICIAN

THE COLONIZER OF DREAMS

We are raised to honor all the wrong explorers and discoverers —thieves planting flags, murderers carrying crosses. Let us at last praise the colonizers of dreams.

—Peter S. Beagle, in his foreword to
The Fellowship of the Ring

That quote is probably one of my favorite quotes in the world; I remember writing it on my notebook in junior-year Honors English. The last two lines hold a great deal of power for me, given my original decision to find another religious answer was based on my revulsion at those "murderers carrying crosses." (I may be the only person who lost faith in Christianity not in church but in history class. Then again, maybe not.) I knew then what I wanted to be; I wanted to be one of those colonizers of dreams. I wanted to shout "Why?" at the Universe, to ask why things couldn't be different.

Now, pushing forty, I find in myself the same desire, the same dream. And it is my inner Magician that moves me to be so. If the Craftsman builds, the Magician changes; and in that change, the world changes. The Magician is the point of transformation.

The Magician is also—and this point may be more important—the keeper of knowledge not within the normal person's ken. This means that the traditional view of the Magician—the bearded wizard who is the master of arcane knowledge, rare arts, and dead languages, the guy who has a stuffed alligator hanging from his rafters and a small imp in a jar in the kitchen—is a valid one. This *also* means that the computer security specialist, the chef who can hand-whip a hollandaise, the weaver who can weave a cloak, the painter, the musician, the historian—they all share in the Magician archetype. In truth, Clarke's Law holds: any sufficiently advanced technology is indistinguishable from magick because any sufficiently advanced technology *is* magick.

Yet there are very few men who would call themselves magicians, other than the guys with doves and assistants wearing little other than sequins. Why? I think it has to do with yin and yang, active and passive, and the expectations that society puts on us to be "real men." Real men do manly things—we weld pipes, rebuild engines, lay sheetrock, raise cattle. We don't bake scones, play cello, or write books on Venetian stained glass. Those are, in two words, sissy things— or at least they were for a very long time.

In recent years, though, things have changed somewhat, and the Magician is flexing his brain again and reentering the world in an active mode. I think it's no mistake that despite the best efforts of some people, the world is becoming a more tolerant place. Yes, there is backlash. Yes, we still have miles to go before we can relax. But the world is changing, and the Magician is at the heart of it.

So why is the Magician archetype so threatening to traditional manhood? I think it's because the Magician is neither, both, all. The traditional view of the Magician archetype was androgynous, both male and female. He was the keeper of secrets, the master of all kinds of magick. Spiritual traditions as widely varied as Congolese, Indian, East Asian, Native

American, and Northern European have revered and honored the cross-dressing or transgendered magician or shaman.

Needless to say, behavior such as this is a huge threat to the traditional image of the male. And I'm not saying that all Magicians are cross-dressers (though, admittedly, Merlin would look *fabulous* in a hot pink mini). But the Magician is willing to step outside his own definition of self and use that power to change the world around him—a step that many men are scared of.

The Tale of Gandalf

Nope, I fibbed. I'm not going to tell a tale of Gandalf. That tale has already been told, and I refuse to even consider that I'm worthy to polish J. R. R. Tolkien's eighth-best pen nib. If you don't know the story of Gandalf, run—don't walk— down to your library, check out *The Hobbit* and *The Lord of the Rings*, and read them. They are, in my humble opinion, some of the greatest works of English literature ever.

The summary, though, is this: Gandalf is the one Wizard sent to Middle-earth in the Third Age who is faithful to his trust. Originally a Maiar, the entities who act as helpers and companions to the Valar, Tolkien's gods, Gandalf the Grey, Saruman the White, Radagast the Brown, and Alatar and Pallando the Blue took human form in order to protect the mortal races from Sauron, a twisted Maiar who desired dominion over all of Middle-earth. Eventually the other four Wizards betrayed or ignored their trust—Saruman gave in to Sauron's power, Alatar and Pallando gave in to mortal power, and Radagast turned his back on mortals in order to concern himself with animals and growing things. Gandalf alone remained true, and his sacrifice in Moria and return as Gandalf the White meant that only he, in the end, was faithful to his mission and nature.

I think that Gandalf's nature as Magician is even more apparent in Sir Ian McKellen's brilliant performance in Peter Jackson's Oscar-winning *Lord of the Rings* trilogy. In the beginning, McKellen plays Gandalf true to the books—quite disreputable and more than a little ragged, to tell the truth. Gandalf comes off like the kind of person who's likely to steal your cat and have it for lunch while he's plundering your garden for potion ingredients and soup makings. By the end of the trilogy, though, he's a supernatural juggernaut in blinding white, defying evil and defending mortality against something too dark to comprehend.

For me, there's some lesson in the fact that McKellen is openly gay in real life. Gandalf goes from slightly dotty to demigod-like in the space of three movies, on one hand dispensing wisdom and on the other hand kicking ass—all played by a man who is, in his own way, a reflection of the traditional Magician archetype. McKellen rather single-handedly dismisses any lingering prejudice that one might have about gay men being pacifist, weakling, or nelly—yet still he has the sensitivity and the supernatural awareness that one would expect from a great magician. (He kicks even more ass as Magneto, but that's another movie.)

The fact is, Gandalf is not a nice person. He's not a whimsical wizard. He has a serious hard edge, and he's more than willing to use it. His redemption of Théoden and how he deals with Gríma Wormtongue, his defiance of Denethor, and the audacious plan to ride into Mordor to certain death to buy Frodo time are all the actions of a man who doesn't coddle or soften the truth. The Magician gives truth; it's not necessarily his desire to make it likable, palatable, or soft and comfy. To seek the Magician's counsel within yourself, to evoke that archetype, means that you're willing to take whatever comes.

Gandalf's lesson, in the end, is that while you may wear varying faces, you must still bear in mind your essential mission and purpose in life. In chapter IX, we talked about discovering a mission in life: that it comes out of a deep need from your childhood and that it fills that need. In Kauth's work on mission, he also states that a mission should be unachievable in one's lifetime; it should be big, grandiose, sweeping. My mission, for example, reads as follows:[35]

> *My mission is to free the present from the chains of the past through education, empowerment, and example.*

Missions usually have central themes. Mine is liberation, freedom, fighting prejudice. Other men may have other missions. Gandalf actually completes his, but it's only managed because he stays completely true to his nature. (He's also a supernatural being, so don't feel inadequate or anything.) We're not talking about external nature, obviously, as Gandalf's fashion sense goes from shabby to Oxydol white in the space of three movies. We're talking about inner nature. To stay true to your nature is to stay true to yourself; to stay true to yourself is to stay true to your nature.

---

35. At least right now. Missions and mission statements can change, based on how people change.

The Tale of Thoth

Thoth is, in Egyptian belief, the god of wisdom, writing, numbers, magick, and all forms of arcane and vital knowledge. In this he represents the voice and spoken word; the ability to do magick and to extend one's will on the world falls within his provenance, and he taught those arts to humankind.

Thoth is the great mediator, the keeper of the balance. His constant role through Egyptian myths is that of the balance between good and evil; three times he has been the point of balance between warring gods, and each time he has kept the battle running in the way it was supposed to run to maintain cosmic order.

When Set dismembered Osiris, Thoth provided Isis with the knowledge to re-create Osiris in order to be sure the cycle of life continued. Thoth is even willing to use unorthodox problem-solving to maintain that cosmic order; when Nut was unable to bear her children in the current calendar, he gambled with the moon and won five more days in the year, allowing their birth. He is the lord of the written word, and all knowledge is recorded by Thoth.

In the later years of Egypt, Thoth became identified with the Hellenic god Hermes, and together they became the patron of medieval and Renaissance magicians. As such, the Tarot deck is often called the Book of Thoth.

In Thoth, we see the Magician as the guardian of cosmic order and the problem solver. Now these are two different faces, but they do overlap in some places; part of keeping the balance in all things requires one to know as much as possible about everything. You should forgive the pun, but Thoth is a manifestation of the balancing act of action and reaction.

What I always find interesting is how Thoth seems to step outside the boundaries of conventional ethics. He is called forth three times to arbitrate the struggle between "good" and "evil"—yet he is always aware that those are just labels, terms that we hang on our own views of the situation. While Set (who plays the villain in two of the three conflicts) is viewed as evil, he really isn't; he is instead the force of destruction, and as such must be a part of the whole equation. Neither creation nor destruction can exist out of balance, or the situation becomes untenable. Thoth as Magician is aware of that, and he acts to maintain that balance as necessary.

While this kind of cosmic awareness is one of Thoth's hallmarks, there is also the side of him that loves to solve problems. When confronted with a challenge, Thoth looks for the most elegant and creative solution as well as the most effective. Through that he expands and utilizes his knowledge and awareness. Thoth is a god for any man who sweats and swears over the *New York Times* crossword puzzle or a copy of *Games* magazine. If there's a drawback to that streak in him and in us, it's that sometimes we don't see the simple solution while looking for the stylish one. Sometimes the best treatment for a Gordian knot *is* a gladius.

Thoth's lesson for us is twofold. First, Thoth exemplifies the delight in the game, the challenge, the mental calisthenics. Thoth stands with any man who competes with his mind, be it chess, Texas hold 'em, Dungeons and Dragons, or fantasy baseball. Our ability as men to store massive amounts of data and to use it to competitive ends falls under Thoth's blessing. (I speak from experience, being a gamer geek from way, way back.) That tendency in us is something we can celebrate and be fully alive in—we can play, we can bluff, and we can win.

Secondly—and perhaps even more importantly—Thoth is the awareness of the balance. A thread that has run throughout this work is that as men we are out of balance due to the demands, roles, and programming put upon us by centuries of patriarchy. Thoth counsels us to step back, evaluate the situation, stop seeing everything in shades of black and white. He is the master of the measured response, the calm demeanor, and the acceptance of both creation and destruction in our own lives.

Yet while we may be masters (or apprentices) of the measured response, we should probably also make sure we have some ability to express and determine our own emotions.

The Tale of Väinämöinen

Väinämöinen is the central character of the great Finnish epic the Kalevala. He is a great sage and wizard, the old wise man who holds many secrets; he has the knowledge of the ages because he was in the womb of his mother, the primal goddess Ilmatar, for seven hundred and thirty years. His voice can charm both woodland creatures and men; he sinks his rival, Joukahainen, into a bog merely by singing him into the ground. He is a master of the kantele, the bell-like harp that Väinämöinen himself invented.

Yet . . . Väinämöinen is oddly awkward in how he interacts with people. When he wins Aino, the sister of

Joukahainen, for a bride, she drowns herself rather than marry him. He founds the land of Kaleva, but his dealings with finding a wife eventually plunge it into enmity with the land of darkness, Pohjola. He buys his freedom from Louha with Ilmarinen's Sampo, but then steals it back.

In the end, the maiden Marjatta eats a berry and gives birth to a baby without a father. When the baby is brought to Väinämöinen to consider, he declares that it should be put to death for such an unnatural birth. The child, only two weeks old, begins to speak of Väinämöinen's many sins and failings, including the death of Aino. Shamed, Väinämöinen goes to the edge of the sea and sings himself a copper boat with which he sails away from the mortal realms, saying he will return when his crafts are needed again.

First thought: I really think that the heroes of the *Kalevala* desperately needed a good online dating service.

Once that little moment of whimsy is over, I see one thing: Väinämöinen is an absolute personification of the greatest pitfall the Magician can fall into.

Let's drop back and look at things for a moment. What do the following people have in common?

- A hardcore computer support person or system administrator

- A professor of some arcane academic discipline

- And a follower of serious and theoretical occult practice

My answer is simple: all of them have a stereotypical reputation for being, shall we say, socially inept. Unskilled at human interaction. Geeks.

The Magician's biggest weakness is that he can fail—*we* can fail—to understand people. I speak from experience: for a long time I was utterly unable to see some of the damage my actions and attitudes were doing to others because I was so wrapped up in my own head most of the time. When I am that far lost in my own cerebral meanderings, I can't get in touch with emotions, either my own or those of others.

The important thing to remember when calling on your Magician archetype is to make sure it stays in balance with the Lover or the Healer. Make sure you stay in your heart as well as in your head. I know I function best when I am standing strong in both places; part of the work we do with the ManKind Project is to make sure men stay in their hearts when they're talking about how they feel, instead of trying to analyze their emotions with their intellects. When I'm analyzing, I'm not experiencing—and often that experience is vital to understanding and accepting.

In the last stanza of the *Kalevala*, the child who forces accountability on Väinämöinen is baptized and becomes the king of Kaleva. Many scholars of mythology tend to turn this into a parable on the rise of Christianity over paganism in Finland. While I acknowledge that's a valid point, I tend to view the end of the *Kalevala* as more of a parable on integrity. Väinämöinen is finally forced to consider his own hubris unflinchingly, and it's not a pretty picture. Like any true magician, he chooses to take time to consider his own folly and spiritual growth. He leaves the option of return open, but knows that as he is he is not truly functional either as magician or man.

Sounds good, right? Here's my question. Why leave in the first place?

If I am in a situation in which I have made a critical emotional error and done damage to someone, my first tendency is to try to run away so that I don't have to deal with the consequences of my own actions. I think this is common to most men; not only do we cause emotional upheaval due to our own remoteness, but we also don't stick around to review—or control—the damage. We have to be accountable for our own action or inaction—otherwise, we fall into Väinämöinen's trap, and in the end when we're faced with our own mistakes we become paralyzed. What we need to do is stay with our mistakes, stay with our feelings, and breathe through them to come out the other side. Only then do we become the full reflection of the Magician—capable, emotional, practical, and accomplished.

In the tale of Ilmarinen, Väinämöinen refused the gift (?) of the metal woman Ilmarinen had made. I find it interesting that the woman who was refused because of her inability to feel— her coldness—was herself gifted to the wizard whose lack of feeling and empathy was brought home to him at the end.

For Further Thought

Am I willing to take whatever comes if I ask for counsel?

Are my responses in balance, instead of seeing the world in extremes?

Am I in my heart, listening to my emotions?

MAGICKAL WORKING

Solving the Enigma

As we've seen, the Magician is, in many ways, all about solving a riddle, meeting a challenge, gaining knowledge. We have also seen the traditional pairing of the Magician, in his embodiment as Thoth, with the Tarot, the traditional fortune-telling cards that have been used for divination for hundreds of years.

It seems that this is a good time to come up with a Tarot layout for men's work. Some notes, however, about Tarot before we begin . . . wait, better idea! Without further ado, I present *Dag's Useful Tarot FAQ*:

Q: Which Tarot deck should I use?

A: Great question. Given that there are approximately seven billion different Tarot decks in existence, including one for any special interest you can imagine, there's a lot of variety available. (And I'm not making fun of special-interest Tarot decks: my current deck is Workman Publishing's *Baseball Tarot*, and I love it.)

What it really comes down to is: what's right for you? My recommendation is to take as many opportunities as you can to look at decks, handle them if possible (but see the etiquette question on the next page), and see how they feel. In my experience, different decks have different personalities—and when you combine that with things like art style and ease of use, there are a lot of variables to play with.

Q: What do you mean, different personalities? Are Tarot decks alive? Are they like Ouija boards? Am I going to be taken over by my Tarot deck?

A: First off, stop hyperventilating and take your St. John's wort.

Now, to answer your question: sort of. I have known Tarot decks and other forms of divination to develop what I can only call a spiritual presence. (Brian Froud's Faerie Oracle, my other regular divination tool, is a great example of same.) When you add that to the fact that divination is, by its nature, a means to link the conscious mind to the deep unconscious, sometimes it can feel as if you have another mind present, answering questions. That's not anything to fear. When you divine, you're looking for answers your conscious mind doesn't have. Sometimes those answers are already present in your subconscious, and they get escorted to your awareness by the symbolism of the divination tool.

In short, relax. More people have been taken over by an insane and unethical desire for money and power or by commercial advertising in the last week than have ever been controlled by a magickal tool.

Q: What's this about Tarot card etiquette?

A: Some people don't allow anyone other than themselves to handle their Tarot cards or divination tools. That's okay; it's a question of personal boundaries, and those are always safe. In general, before you touch someone else's tools, ask.

Q: How do I take care of my Tarot deck?

A: Keep them in something. I use a drawstring bag to keep dirt and wear and tear off of mine; some people use a small flat box. The original box the deck came in is all well and good for a while, but consider that it's probably made of cardboard and cardboard wears, especially on the corners.

It's also very common to carry around a cloth to do your readings on. This is both a great magickal focus (the cloth itself can become sacred space) and a practical way of taking care of your cards.

Now—the Men's Tarot Layout.

Gold	Elder	Shadow
Magician	Outcome	Youth
	Warrior	

This Tarot layout is based on some of the archetypes that have been examined in this book. There are actually two versions: a seven-card version and a eleven-card version.

In the seven-card version:

1. The Youth—This card represents the beginning of the question. What early influences are on it? Where did it stem out of? What, if anything, was the initiator of the situation at hand?

2. The Warrior—The current tenor of the situation. What influences and actions are being taken by the current people involved? What is acting on the situation?

3. The Magician—What are the unseen forces in the current situation? What haven't you thought of or accounted for? What external forces may be affecting the situation?

4. The Elder—What is the history behind the situation? What may be resurfacing from the past that's coming into play again?

5. Gold—What positive influences are in play? What is your best tool, action, feeling, or influence that you can bring to bear to achieve your desired outcome?

6. Shadow—What are the negative influences in play? What part of yourself and others may be holding you back from achieving your goal?

7. Outcome—What is the most likely outcome of the situation if nothing changes between now and the moment of resolution?

The eleven-card reading uses these seven cards and adds four more positions for further detail:

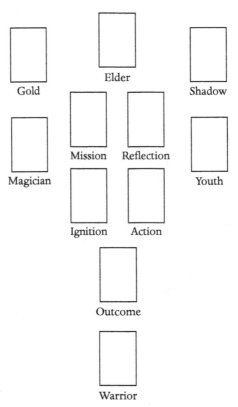

1. Youth

2. Warrior

3. Magician

4. Elder

5. Gold

6. Shadow

7. Mission—How does this question relate to mission, either yours or someone else's? What mission is or is not being achieved by this situation? What part of the little boy's deepest needs are or are not being met?

8. Reflection—What feminine influences—literal, spiritual, or metaphorical—are involved in the situation?

9. Ignition—What is the single point on which the entire situation hangs? What's the balance point of all the influences involved?

10. Action—What can be done to move that ignition point in the desired direction?

11. Outcome

RITUAL OF AFFIRMATION

Rite of Self-Initiation

Unlike our other rituals so far, this is a rite of self-initiation. Now I admit to having a strong preference for group work, both in men's work and in more traditional Pagan circles and covens. I believe that solitary work is missing one very important element: I think it's hard to get real feedback when the only mirror you have is yourself. That said, however, I realize the realities of the situation; if you're somewhere remote where there just aren't people around to help you with your work, then you sometimes have to go it alone.

This isn't really a self-initiation for men's work; for that, I would recommend the ManKind Project (www.mkp.org)

and their New Warrior Training Adventure weekend.[36] What this ritual is designed for is a self-initiation as a spiritual seeker, a Magician, whatever you think is appropriate to a path of spiritual growth.

A simple altar should be laid with a God and Goddess candle, quarter candles, and symbols of the elements: a wand, a blade, a cup, and a stone. There should also be a central candle, a pillar of a color that seems representative of the path the seeker is taking. Other altar accoutrements may include pictures of ancestors, spiritual influences, or other sacred objects as desired. All speaking parts refer to the man doing the ritual; by definition, this is a ritual done alone.

Light the four quarter candles:

> I welcome the Air of the East, the direction of knowledge.
> I welcome the Fire of the South, the direction of power.
> I welcome the Water of the West, the direction of wisdom.
> I welcome the Earth of the North, the direction of strength.

Light the God candle:

---

36. I accept that by now you may be counting the references to MKP and the NWTA with a slightly bemused air. All I can say to that is *it saved my life and I believe in it.* It has made me a more effective man, a more effective priest, and has given me the guts to go ahead and write this. If one man does the weekend because of this book, I will have achieved one of my goals in writing it. (And if that man contacts me, if any man contacts me saying he signed up for the NWTA because of my work, I'll try to staff his weekend—providing I can get there and that real life allows me to do so. I'm that serious about the work.)

I welcome the God in his face as the Magician. The initiator, the keeper of mysteries, the giver of wisdom and truth. May he guide my hand tonight.

Light the Goddess candle:

> I welcome the Great Mother, the Goddess, mirror of mankind and eternal keeper of mysteries. May she light my way tonight.

Sit and ground and center for a moment, listening to the silence and your breathing.

> Tonight is the beginning of a journey—I declare it.
> Tonight I begin to look for something hidden—I declare it.
> Tonight I reach for something more within myself—I declare it.
> This is the moment where I step forth.
> The Fool on the road, knowing that this is both journey's beginning
> And journey's end.
> I go forth to seek something more than what I have known.
> I swear to myself to be honest and open to whatever truth I find.
> I swear to myself that if I am given or I find abilities beyond what I have,
> I will use them for the greater good, harming as little as I can.
> I swear to see the Divine in the face of everyone I meet,

To walk in a sacred manner because we live in a sacred
world.

I swear to keep my word if given, to remain silent if
sworn to.

I swear to protect those who ask it of me with a good
heart.

I swear to remain open to the Infinite, within and without.

*At this point, further oaths may be taken if the candidate desires.
The candle is then lit.*

This candle represents my desire for enlightenment.
May it always guide me during moments of darkness.
I will bear in mind the watchword of the Magician:
interconnectedness. May I understand that all things
are interconnected, and I am not truly separate from
the world around me.

*The candidate may, at this time, extinguish the quarter candles
with an appropriate thank-you to the elements. Remain meditating
on the central candle for a period of time.*

XI

THE DESTROYER

ENTROPY TRUMPS EVERYTHING

Pale Death with impartial tread beats at the poor man's cottage door and at the palaces of kings.

—Horace, *Odes*

It's always a good idea to start a chapter with a nice bleak quote guaranteed to make your reader throw up his hands in despair and futility, right? But let's face the truth: that quote from Horace is indeed true. Death is an equal opportunity destroyer. Everything ends.

And if everything didn't end, there'd be no room for anything new. The cycle of creation and destruction has to be a cycle. There has to be a food chain, and someone has to eat or be eaten every day. As a society, we try to distance ourselves from the reality of that situation—meat comes in neat packages and we never see the knacker's hammer come down on the cow's head. Anything worn out or less than perfect is speedily dealt with, and we're advised to consume, consume, consume—to get this year's model, replace anything already used a little, and avoid the harsh reality of dwindling resources and starving children. We pretend the Destroyer doesn't exist, when he is all around us every day.

What are we afraid of? In a word: death. The Destroyer is death, ending, finality—and for all of our religious faith and belief in past lives and continuing beyond the abandonment of our current mortal shells, we don't really *know*, do we, what happens after that last breath? Faith isn't much comfort sometimes. And so we run from the Destroyer. We pretend he and his do not exist—and we think we're safe until he comes for us, and we find out he's been there all along.

Of course, there's always the other option. We can revel in death and destruction. We can create an attitude that we're born to raise hell, meaner than Death himself, ready to fight and kill at a moment's notice. We can develop fascinations. We can lose ourselves in portrayed violence and stage blood. We can stop taking care of ourselves—and take foolish risks and try to live out destruction in ourselves. Either way, we're talking about men who are sadly out of balance and don't even realize it.

Death is the one inevitability. (You can, indeed, get out of taxes. Just ask Enron.) And death is also really the primal fear; most other fears are a fear of death in disguise. (I'm afraid of falling, but I suspect it's not the fall but the sudden stop at the end that really gets me on a visceral, fight-or-flight level.) Men seem, in my experience, to be particularly vulnerable to a fear of death—or at least a fear of dying before they make some sort of mark on the world. So we continue in a back-and-forth dance: some of us desperately afraid of death and some of us embracing it to the extent of folly but never really coming to terms with it, finding peace with it, accepting it when the time comes.

The Destroyer archetype is Death. But rather than the Christian concept of the Grim Reaper, who cuts you down and leaves you there until some mythical Judgment Day, the Destroyer destroys so that the Creator can create. Neither can exist without the other. We see this reflected in nature as well; trees fall and rot into soil and new trees are born. Animals die and go to feed scavengers who themselves play roles in the ecosystem that allow the animals to continue growing and living. It is an inescapable truth—and a truth that as men we're incredibly inept at applying to ourselves.

Destruction must occur. The seasons turn, the Nile floods, the crops grow and die—but the desert goes on. Just ask Set.

The Tale of Set

You do not know me.

You may think you know me, but you do not. You have heard the stories: how I killed my brother Osiris, scattered his body, usurped his throne. How it took trickery by Isis and a decision by Ra to force me to give up the throne, and how in that decision my enmity with Horus, my nephew, was created. Mortals call me evil. I am a convenient villain—fratricide, false Pharaoh, caricature of the night, lord of demons, spirit of destruction.

As with most things, the truth is never that simple.

Do you know that every night my father, Ra, sails his solar barge through the underworld, and I stand on its bow and protect it from Apep, the serpent who devours all things? Do you know that I am the spirit of the desert that encroaches upon the green valley of the Nile, and as such restrain it in its proper place? And have you considered that without my intervention, Osiris could not rule as the lord of the dead and bring hope to those who die that they may be born again in their proper time?

Have you ever felt the fury of the unbridled sand-storm? Do you know the secrets of the scorpion and the vulture, the truths written in dune and dust devil? I am the lord of Lower Egypt, and I have laid the crown upon the Pharaoh's brow.

I am destruction in name and in spirit, but it is destruction that is necessary and destruction that causes change. I am the enemy of stagnation; I am the eternal spirit of rebellion that questions the current order. I am shadow to the light of Horus, and neither of us would be visible without the other.

I am Set. And you do not know me.

Set's tale gives us our main lesson right off the bat; our interpretation of classical mythology tends to classify the gods into black and white, and the truth is rarely that simple. Much like people, unvarnished and uncomplicated good and evil are rare commodities; one might even say nonexistent in the real scheme of things. Yes, Set commits fratricide—but in one light it may be inevitable fratricide that maintains the natural order and provides Osiris with his guidance into his next divine incarnation.

I'm not advocating fratricide. (I kinda like my brothers, truth be known.) Nevertheless, the truth remains that the Destroyer's motivation is not always easy to classify, especially in the framework of our understanding and our fears. In Set's case, his actions seem to be to be guarding the natural order—light and dark, life and death, desert and river.

There's a huge piece of wisdom that we can take from this. The Destroyer, at its heart, is about duty: to the order of the Universe, to the cycle of rebirth, to doing what needs to be done to make sure that things continue the way they're supposed to go. It's not a pretty job, and it's rarely a popular one; in Set's case, it means that he has to take actions that most "right-thinking" people consider repugnant. The Destroyer is, by his nature, unyielding; there is no room for mercy in his worldview, because the greater compassion of keeping cosmic order and cycles has to be maintained.

The fear of death is a constant thread in human thought. Psychiatrists try to explain it through birth trauma, Buddhists try to avoid it through achieving the death of ego, and artists ranging from filmmakers to poets have made it the central theme of tens of thousands of works of art. My conjecture, for what it's worth, is that we fear death because death is implacable. Death cannot be bought off, negotiated with, or threatened. We can come up with new tools to buy ourselves some time, but when the call comes, it comes—and everything you might have saved up or earned will mean nothing. Factor in the reality that we live in a world in which, given an hour's effort, death could come knocking for millions of us at once, and it's no wonder we're frightened by the implacability of the Destroyer. In an era of nuclear weapons and looming ecological catastrophe, we're doing a great job in taking over the Destroyer's job without maintaining his concern for balance.

So how do we, as men, deal with the fear of death? As with many things, we can turn our fear into a strength by embracing the very thing that we fear. We can be "bloody, bold, and resolute," to quote Shakespeare; we can decide to not give up without a fight. We can work to change things. We, too, can be adamantine and unyielding.

The Tale of Hades

I am Hades, the lord of the underworld.

Among the first of the Olympians, I am older brother to Zeus and Poseidon and younger sibling to Hestia, Demeter, and Hera. It is my place to guard the realm of the dead, as Zeus guards the sky and Poseidon the waters.

I have been called evil. I have been accused of trickery in gaining my consort, Persephone. Homer in the Iliad called me "adamantine and unyielding." It is true; I am. I judge the dead without mercy or emotion. I do not allow my subjects to leave my realm, for death must come to all; it is one of the unbreakable rules of the Universe. Those who try to rescue souls from my embrace will fail.

I am not, however, without my gifts. The depths of the earth, which I rule, give forth gold, iron, stone, grain, gems. I am only united with my consort and lady for part of the year, so that winter does not hold the world in its steely embrace all the time. Finally, I am just; no man escapes my touch and my realm, and when I judge a man he is judged with utter and complete equanimity. Unlike some of the other Olympians, my emotions do not color my actions; I am the still point in a chaotic world.

That quote from the *Iliad* really sticks with me. The full quote is: "Why do we loathe Hades more than any god, if not because he is so adamantine and unyielding?"[37] *Loathe* is a pretty strong word. Indeed, with one phrase Homer seems to capture the entire nature of human emotion towards death.

Let's turn it around for a moment, though, and consider this: Hades' constant nature is not something to be reviled but something to be admired, emulated, and embraced. Hades has a charge, and he sticks with it, unlike some of the other Hellenic deities, whose myths portray them as somewhat feckless and more than willing to break the rules when it suits them. Hades does what he says he's going to do. He does whatever it takes to maintain the cycle and keep the Universe moving forward.

Often as men we are afraid to say what we think and to offer other men and other people in our lives the hard edge of our unvarnished judgment; often we are afraid to do whatever it takes in a given situation to achieve the greatest good. Both of those actions require a great deal of Hadean energy to achieve.

The fact is that men are taught to lie to each other. We're taught to be nice. We're taught not to say what we think because we might make each other uncomfortable—or, worse, threaten each other and therefore cause conflict. And as the patriarchal order continues to crumble, the reactionary response says that all conflict is bad and to be avoided.

To which I say, channeling my Hadean nature: *bullshit.*

Men are designed for conflict. In a study he conducted, Dr. Mark van Vugt, a professor at the University of Kent in

---

37. Homer, *The Iliad*, trans. by Samuel Butler (Chicago: Encyclopædia Britannica, 1952). Book IX.

England, reported that "men are more likely to lead groups in more autocratic, militaristic ways than women"[38]—in other words, men are more likely to enjoy dealing with conflict and to thrive on conflict. As coverage of van Vugt's research put it: "'We all know males are more aggressive than females,' van Vugt said, adding that co-operation is needed to establish institutions and governments and to wage wars. 'Male co-operation is a double-edged sword.'"[39]

In other words, as men we cannot avoid conflict. We're bred for it. It's in our brains, our bones, and our balls—so we might as well stop being afraid of it. Part of channeling that conflict into more constructive channels is to start being honest with each other. That's where the unafraid nature of Hades comes in.

In my work in the ManKind Project, I have hundreds of brothers who know my shadows and who are willing to call me on them if the shadows get control of me. I have brothers who will call me on my shit and not let me be out of integrity with myself and others. Those men are not, thank the gods, going to be nice to me. They are going to be blunt, hard-edged—or, if you prefer the Homeric term, adamantine and unyielding. While I decry and abhor the injustices and injuries done in the name of patriarchy—both to women and

---

38. Quoted in Elli Leadbeater, "Why Men at War Will Pull Together," BBC News Online (September 12, 2006), http://news.bbc.co.uk/1/hi/sci/tech/5333794.stm (accessed September 12, 2007).

39. "Media Coverage," *KentPsychologist* newsletter, vol. 1, number 3 (March 2007). Online at www.kent.ac.uk/psychology/department/newsletters/mar2007.pdf (accessed September 10, 2007).

to men—I think that turning ourselves into timid, emasculated boys afraid of our own power and our ability to thrive on conflict is in no way an appropriate response.

That is the lesson we can take from Hades' tale. It's all right to keep a hard edge and not compromise our essential nature. Everything—including the male ability to thrive on conflict—has a place in the natural order of things.

The Tale of Rudra

Rudra is storm and wind and destruction.

Rudra is a face of Shiva, the Hindu god of destruction and creation. He is an old face, a very old face, a grim god who was not even honored among the sacrifices in Vedic society. There are hymns to him, but in them his name is not spoken. He is the Hunter, outside the normal order of the gods. In the Rig Veda, it is said: "We live in dread, and pray that you pass us by."

Rudra is fear.

Yet Rudra also guards the cosmic order, Dharma.[40] *He takes action, swift and sure, against those who flagrantly violate its principles. And when he hears the cries of the wounded and the sorrowful, he provides healing. He is a primal force, too large perhaps to be called a god. He exists*

---

40. "Dharma is generally defined as 'righteousness' or 'duty'. Dharma is the principle of righteousness. It is the principle of holiness. It is also the principle of unity . . . Dharma is the cementer and sustainer of social life. The rules of Dharma have been laid down for regulating the worldly affairs of men. Dharma brings as its consequence happiness, both in this world and in the next." From "Dharma," www.hinduism.co.za/dharma.htm#What%20is%20Dharma (accessed September 5, 2007).

as a manifestation of Dharma and the life that supports it. He lives "an authentic life, with utter disdain for convention."[41]

Rudra is destruction and creation and Dharma.

Rudra is an old, old god. He dates from the Vedic era in India, over 3500 years ago, and there is a certain primal energy and majesty about him. This is not a god that you can cuddle up to and feel all warm and fuzzy; Rudra is power and a destructive and unrestrained power at that. By all rights, he *should* be feared.

But how do we explain the fact that he was also sought for healing? Once again, the puzzling dichotomy of the Destroyer snaps into sharp relief for our examination. The key, as with all of the Destroyers, is the position as the guardian of the natural order, of Dharma. Rudra destroys, Rudra heals. Rudra is the god for everyone who has ever had to take the poison of chemotherapy into their body to fight cancer; Rudra's hand steadies the saw of the military surgeon who amputates a shattered limb. Rudra is called upon to heal because some illnesses, some hurts, some wounds are outside the normal operation of Dharma; some things are not supposed to happen. When they do occur, Rudra is as quick to act and step forward to *protect* as he is to *destroy* when it is destruction that is called for.

This is the mirror of the hard edge we talked about earlier. Sometimes what is called for is the truth, the hard edge,

41. "Shiva—the Oldest God Known to Mankind," IndiaYogi.com, www.indiayogi.com/content/indgods/shiva.asp (accessed May 29, 2007).

the unrelenting counsel, the adamantine face of brother to brother when men tell men when they're being morons. Sometimes what is called for is healing, gentleness, and mercy. This brings us full circle in the Destroyer; the same hard, unyielding energy that destroys can also be used to heal.

It's all in how a wounded man responds to outside stimuli. Sometimes you need to be tough; sometimes you need to let the man mourn and feel his pain and go through it and therefore go out of it. This is the gift of the Destroyer; that energy is equally facile at either option. All it takes is discernment to determine the best way to reach a man and help him deal with his wounds. In time, I have become reasonably competent at it, though there are men I work with in the ManKind Project and in other places who astonish me at just how good they are in reading other men. Whether we challenge or cradle a man, in the end it is the Destroyer who stands behind us and provides us with the energy and blessing to do whatever it takes.

For Further Thought

Am I afraid of taking an action that needs to happen?

Am I speaking my truth, or am I saying what people want to hear?

Am I willing to heal with as much toughness as I put into challenging others?

MAGICKAL WORKING

Documenting the Shadow

As Carl Jung put it: "Everyone carries a shadow, and the less it is embodied in the individual's conscious life, the blacker and denser it is . . . if it is repressed and isolated from consciousness, it never gets corrected."[42]

This is the ritual in which we deal with the things we fear.

We've talked a lot in this chapter about the fact that men fear the Destroyer, men fear death. As part of that fear, all of us have things within ourselves that we don't want to look at too closely—our manifestations of the Jungian concept of shadow, the parts of ourselves we repress or bury. Shadow can be scary stuff; we all have, on some level, our inner demons and darknesses that we don't want to admit to. Shadow can also be constructive; it is the source of our hunches, intuitions, and leaps of logic that we can't always make on the conscious level.

It is my belief that a functional, whole man needs to be in touch with his shadow. We're too dangerous if we have no relationship with it whatsoever, and its quiet whispers can guide us in situations where our conscious, rational face breaks down. The caveat, though, is that shadow work is best done in groups; if it's done alone, it needs to be somewhat remote and passive. So what I'd like to do is do a Shadow Dream Diary.

Recommended Tools

- A blank book with lined pages. Personally, I recommend wide-lined pages for journaling unless you write

---

42. Carl Gustav Jung, *Psychology and Religion* (New Haven, CT: Yale University Press, 1938).

very, very small. Hereafter I'll refer to this book as the "dream book."

- A second blank book. This one can be smaller, as it needs to fit under your pillow while you sleep, and it would be useful—but not necessary—if it had a clasp and lock. Hereafter I'll refer to this book as the "shadow book."

- A vial of cinnamon oil.

For me at least, this isn't really a "cast circle" sort of magickal working. Instead, get yourself into a comfortable, safe space with a good pen and sit down with the shadow book. Carefully anoint the book with a touch of the cinnamon oil—cinnamon is a masculine energy, bright and protective, and will help keep the shadow work you're going to do in that book contained where it belongs. As you rub the oil, repeat the following:

Let this anointing of my shadow's voice.

Bring the shadow I bear into my consciousness.

Let it brighten my mind's vistas

To bring me greater understanding.

In the name of the Destroyer, maintainer of the cosmic order,

So mote it be.

Take a moment and write down three truths about yourself that you wouldn't want to admit to anyone—three of your darkest desires, deepest fears, or greatest shames. Often, deep emotions like this are reflections of your shadow, so bear that in mind as you write. Once you are finished, lock the book (if it has a lock) and leave it be for a while.

On the same night, put the shadow book under your pillow. (If the smell of cinnamon will keep you from sleeping, feel free to substitute any other protective oil, or use none at all.) Put the dream book along with a pen near your bed and sleep as normal.

You may have strong dreams relating to your shadow that night (in fact, the whole purpose of this working is to have that happen). Journal them in the dream book. Sleep on these three "shadow truths" for three nights, and then write down three more and continue the process.

Every so often, go back over your dream book. Is there some message that keeps coming up for you in this? Is your shadow trying to communicate something?

Ritual of Affirmation

The Circle of Truth

The Circle of Truth is not a ritual to be undertaken lightly. It is designed to provide a man with guidance and wisdom when he's stuck. Before I lay out the ritual, I want to be sure some ground rules are understood:

1. The man who is the center of the ritual must be willing to accept that he is going to hear some tough truths about himself, some things that he may not like. If a man is not willing to make that stretch, then *don't do it*. It's that simple.

2. The men who are making up the circle must be willing to be honest without being cruel or vindictive.

They must also agree to stick to the subject. The man who asks for the Circle of Truth is the man in control, subject to the Elder's administration of the process.

3. The Elder in charge of the circle must be willing to take control of the situation if it appears to be out of control in any way. If the man at the center of the circle breaks down or becomes defensive, if the men on the outside become ego-invested and fall into their own shadows, or if the entire process stalemates, the Elder must change the energy or, if necessary, terminate the process.

4. No man may speak without the talking stick except the Elder. This is an absolute in order to keep the circle from descending into chaos. Also, no man may be present who is not actively participating.

5. The timekeeper's word is law, save when the Elder makes changes to the circle's flow.

6. If every man present agrees, this is a good ritual to record so that the candidate can go back and go over the information and feedback he receives.

For this ritual, there is no altar. If at all possible, men should sit on the floor to remain grounded; arranging them in a halfcircle or three-quarter circle around the man is the best option, with the Elder facing the man at the bottom of the circle.

Opposite the Elder, there should be a low table with implements for grounding energy; stones like hematite, a basin of salt water, smudge, and whatever else the Elder thinks wise to have on hand for taking care of the men participating in the ritual. There should also be a loaf of bread, a dish of salt, and a chalice of water. The Elder should also have a clearly indicated talking stick. A man should be asked to step in as timekeeper; he, like the Elder, does not participate in any other capacity.

Finally, there should be a man who is not part of the ritual preparing the cleansing cloths. (See page 260 in appendix I.)

Elder: I bless this space in the name of the Air of wisdom, the Fire of truth, the Water of healing, and the Earth of grounding. May it contain our shadow and our light, and may we remember we are in sacred space.

Men acknowledge.

Elder: I bless this bread and this cup as a symbol of the community we share. Though we may walk through darkness together, we are always brothers.

Men acknowledge.

Elder: I bless this space in the name of the Destroyer, the god who clears our preconceptions and maintains the cycle of life. I also bless this space in the name of the Dark Mother, whom all come to in the end. May She bless us with the truth.

Men acknowledge. Elder turns to the candidate.

Elder: This man has chosen to step forward and pass the ordeal of the Circle of Truth. He is to be honored for his courage; it is a difficult and frightening place to stand before a group of men knowing you are to be confronted with your own shadows.

(To the man) What is the shadow or question that you want this group to specifically offer you wisdom on?

The candidate presents his quandary to the group. The Circle of Truth is designed to offer feedback on a specific question: "What should I do about my failing marriage?" "Why can't I seem to get ahead at work?" "Why can't I stay faithful?"

> **Elder:** Are you ready to hear whatever comes? You may accept it or reject it as you choose—some of it may be truth for you, some of it may be projection from other men's shadows—but you need to hear it, and reject or accept it consciously.

The man acknowledges his readiness. The Elder hands the talking stick to the first man in the circle to his left.

It is time to begin. The first man may now speak.

At this time, the Circle of Truth progresses around the circle of men. Each man's turn in the Circle follows a specific format:

1. *The man offering feedback has one minute to ask for additional data about the situation.*
2. *The man offering feedback then has two to three minutes to speak.*
3. *The man in the center has one minute to answer or comment if he so chooses. This continues around the circle.*

As each man finishes, he steps to the altar and purifies and cleanses himself as he chooses. When finished, he should rejoin the circle unless his own shadow or psychic baggage means it is best for him to step out of the circle. Men should be strongly discouraged from leaving the room and disrupting the sacred space.

When the circle is finished, the Elder takes the talking stick and maintains silence for a time, letting men come down from the energy. During this period of silence, a man hands out the cleansing cloths and the men cleanse themselves.

After a time, the Elder speaks to the candidate:

Elder: Are you complete in this Circle of Truth?
The man either acknowledges so, or his concern is handled free-form.
Elder: Then, as the ancestors in many cultures have done, we share bread, salt, and water, to remind ourselves that we are a community.
The bread, salt, and cup are passed.
Elder: I commend to you the watchword of the Destroyer: *entropy.* Bear in mind, all who hear this, that any man may fall prey to his shadow without constant vigilance and care.
(To the directions as he speaks) The Earth of determination, the Water of love, the Fire of the spirit, and the Air of wisdom; we thank and bless their spirits, knowing they are with us always.
Elder: We thank the Great Goddess, She who is our other soul, for standing with us tonight. We thank the Great God, He who is our root and our spirit, for standing with us tonight. Go now and begin your journey. We are with you always; come to us should you need our wisdom.

XII

THE KING

THE SOVEREIGN OF DESIRE

I am, indeed, a king,
because I know how to rule myself.

—Pietro Aretino

In modern American society if you say "the King" to most men, they'll wonder where Elvis has been sighted this week. This is, to me, a perfect definition of tragedy. It's not that I have anything in particular against Elvis—his pre-Las Vegas music is cool, and *Bubba Ho-tep* is a work of sheer cinematic genius—but kingship deserves much, much better.

The archetype of the mature male has taken some hits over the years. From buttons saying "Don't Trust Anyone Over 30" to Michael Moore talking about stupid white men, the mature and powerful male who was a respected authority figure in the 1950s is now the punch line of a bad joke in the aughts—and, sad to say, the loss in prestige and reputation has been deserved.

The mature male establishment[43] has, since 1964, given us Vietnam, Iraq I (We Won! Let's Leave The Same Guy In Charge), Iraq II (We Were Supposed To Win This Quickly, Not Die A Whole Lot), the hole in the ozone layer, Chernobyl, Three Mile Island, the destruction of the rain forest,

---

43. When I use this term, I mean The Establishment. The Man. The Con. And yes, that mostly means white men; as a white man, I accept that. I just don't want to get into the racial issue further than that. The Establishment victimizes all of us.

and various other commercial and social intolerances that have resulted in a loss of faith in the Establishment. Hierarchies and mature male energy is a little punch-drunk, and no matter how many Bohemian Grove and Skull and Bones members try to pretend otherwise, things are going downhill.

This is all well and good. But perhaps we're throwing the baby out with the bathwater when we let the Establishment drag the mature male archetype down with it.

Myths, legends, and stories from time immemorial have spoken of the majesty and power of the King. Whether his name is Arthur, Barbarossa, Gandhi, Charlemagne, Shaka, John Adams, Cesar Chavez, King, or any one of myriad others, he is the symbol for power, change, and regal nobility. He is a leader, a firebrand, and above all not a youth or a feckless fool but rather a mature male upright in his full power and wisdom. The King is the primal force for benevolence and strength in the world, and he's had a bit of a hard time of it recently. It is time to change that.

The Tale of Jupiter

I am Jupiter, king of the Roman gods. It is easy to equate me with Zeus, king of the Hellenic deities—and yes, there are some great similarities between us, just as Hellenic society helped shape the glory that was Rome.

But there is a difference you should bear in mind. The Greek gods and goddesses were anthropomorphic. They had human loves, desires, hates, fears, and motivations. The Hellenic myths are about gods and men.

By contrast, my myths and my stories are about the state. The tales of Aeneas, Remus and Romulus, and the founding of the great city on the seven hills were and are the myths of Rome. I, Jupiter, am not a human in godly guise, but rather the soul and spirit of Rome. I am the guardian of the law and the embodiment of the Empire. I was worshiped on the Capitoline Hill with Juno and Minerva as the primary deities of Rome. There are no stories about my chasing of nymphs or dallying with mortals. Rome had her light and dark moments—great triumphs, hideous crimes and evils—but whatever else she was, she remained strong. I, Jupiter, was and am that strength, the strength of the law and of the state.

Stories and myths are well and good in their place. But I am Jupiter Optimus Maximus, the best and greatest; Jupiter Victor, the leader of victorious armies; and Jupiter Caelestis, the heavenly one, the great King and Emperor whose divine glory ignited the glory of Rome.

If you're getting the impression that Jupiter is more of a primal force than an approachable god, you're getting the right idea. Jupiter is and was Rome; one cannot be extricated from the other. This is the King at his most essential: the living personification of the State, the Kingdom, the Empire. Jupiter is the guide who led Rome from Trojan refugees stumbling ashore to an empire that stretched from Northumberland to Persia.

With Jupiter's example, we see the King clearly. There are times when the King merely exists to be a symbol for the work of his subjects, and times when the King's mere presence empowers and enlightens people to greater effort and greater success. While there's no way to know if the legions of Rome would have been as successful without the inspiration of Jupiter Victor, his presence and blessing helped them conquer most of the known world at the time.

As we learn to channel our inner King, we realize that the King is often in a contemplative or symbolic role. Yes, at times he's active, riding, taking the field against his enemies, but sometimes it's enough that men see the King and are ennobled and energized by his presence.

As men, we're often pressured to respond in any situation with action, action, and more action. Our society rarely supports or rewards a man who contemplates the situation before he acts, or who doesn't act at all. Yet we can be in such a hurry to act that we can do exactly the wrong thing.

Here's a great example. My beloved Elisabeth doesn't smile very often. When she does, it's like a spotlight in a darkened room, but her customary expression is pretty solemn. It's a very neutral expression; it's often hard to read. Often I get worried about this—after nine years, you'd think I'd learn—and I get all panicky and ask her, "What's wrong?" Sometimes I even do this repeatedly. By following this truly brilliant course of action I often create "something wrong" when there was nothing wrong to begin with.

I am convinced based on my knowledge of myself and my reactions that my action stems from a desperate need to do *something* when faced with a situation in which I'm not completely in control. It doesn't matter if the something I'm about to do is dumber than a box of rocks; I have some deep-seated gender-linked need to fix any situation with action, and in my experience it's not just me. Most of the social ineptitude to which men are heirs shows up because we open our mouths or take action when we should just relax and let things happen.

This is one of the lessons of the King; sometimes, it's all right to just sit and consider the situation. In fact, often just being there, not doing anything, is actually the answer to the problem. I have been present for a lot of deep healing work with men and women; one of the most important lessons I try to keep in mind every time I participate in that work is to just be present and shut the hell up. If a man needs to cry, or rage, or talk, the worst thing that can be done is to interrupt him with my own stuff. In that, I try to hold on to the energy of the King and just *be*.

In order to be in the moment, we must be honest—honest with ourselves, honest with others, honest in our intentions and in our emotions. We must exist with majesty and benefice, content in the kingdom of the self.

The Tale of the August Personage of Jade

In the myths and tales of Chinese mythology, the name of the keeper of the celestial order changes. From Shangdi, the first name, through Tian, Heaven, and Pangu, the creator of the world out of chaos, the names may change but the spirit remains the same. In the Middle Kingdom, it was the task of the king to bring order out of chaos and blessing out of adversity. No such ruler's stories are as well-known as those of the August Personage of Jade, Yu Huang Shangdi, commonly known as the Jade Emperor.

Born as a prince in a divine kingdom, his light was such that it filled his land. He was kind and generous and wise even as a child. Upon achieving majority, he went off to undergo great trials that resulted in his achieving Golden Immortality and true enlightenment. These took many millions of years, and also undergoing trial was the king of the demons, an evil entity whose intention was to take over Earth and proclaim himself King of the Universe.

When the Jade Emperor finally finished his trials, he emerged from the mountain cave where he had been in retreat, in order to aid mankind and teach skills such as medicine and agriculture. At this time, however, the army of demons, led by the evil one, assaulted Heaven. The Jade Emperor looked up from his labors to find the demons about to overwhelm Heaven. Returning to the aid of the immortals, the Jade Emperor defeated and utterly destroyed the evil one due to his superior cultivation of the Tao. To honor his victory, the assembled gods and immortals proclaimed him the King of All.

What I find interesting about the Jade Emperor is how many male archetypes are present in this simple story. We have the Youth, the Divine Child who fills his kingdom with light; the Magician who spends millions of years gaining mastery over arcane arts; and the Warrior, throwing down the evil one and defeating him. Over all, though, there is the theme of the King, the divine archetype who preserves the establishment and defends humanity from the forces of chaos.

Robert Moore and Douglas Gillette describe the King as the architect of dreams—the mature male empowered to change the world and make it a more benevolent space. Every true King wants to create paradise on Earth for his subjects. This is the vision that every politician and preacher wants us to buy into—that somewhere there's a vision of paradise that's powerful enough for all of us to be a part of, that we can have it if only we buy whatever they're selling.

That's false kingship. The King does not need to convince others of the inherent rightness of his cause, and he certainly doesn't need to sell anything or lie in order to get others to buy into it. The Jade Emperor doesn't worry about whether or not anyone thinks his way is right. He just deals with the problem when it arrives, with his own power, benevolence, and nobility. The false king, on the other hand, lies and uses fear as a weapon.

We all know and have seen politicians who use smear tactics, fear tactics, or out-and-out lies in order to get their way. While I am not going to mention any names in order to maintain some sense of fairness, that particular undercurrent has been a pretty prevalent theme in the world for the last few years. We were told that in order to protect ourselves from terrorists, we must overthrow the government of Iraq, and that the government of Iraq had weapons of mass destruction. Now that the truth appears to have been otherwise, thousands of American dead and tens of thousands of Iraqi dead are on our hands—and no end to the dance of death is in sight. This is the false king in action, and it's not pretty.

The true King, on the other hand, is like the Buddha—he is content to rule the kingdom of self and to focus his energy toward maintaining its integrity and growth. The Jade Emperor may be the acclaimed King of Heaven, but he does not ask for it; he does what he does because it is the right and proper thing to do, in accordance with his own inner desires and inner nature.

While we may not be bodhisattvas, there's a lesson here for us. We can truly channel our inner King by following some simple principles: be honest at all times about what our dreams are and what they mean for other people; seek to know the self and from that seek rulership only over the self; and allow others the same right. It's easy stuff, really, and it's the very reflection of the benevolence of the Jade Emperor and of the King that shines through him.

The Tale of Perun

I am Perun. Hear my thunder! See my lightning!

I am Perun. I am the lord of war and my arrows of stone crack the trees with a mighty flash. I am the lord of rulership and nobility and my name is sworn upon by princes making agreements. Woe betide the faithless prince who breaks his word sworn on my name.

I am Perun. I am the eagle who perches on the highest branch of the sacred tree, and from there I watch my enemy, Veles, the trickster god of the dead and the sea. Our struggle is eternal; he seeks to disrupt the order of things, and I seek to defend it. I may defeat him, but he will return; it is the nature of things. And when princes swear oaths to my name, his is also included.

I am Perun. My symbols are carved on roof beams to protect the houses from my lightning. My golden apples—perhaps what you call "ball lightning"—is the touch of death. But I am the supreme ruler of the gods, and Vladimir the Great raised statues to me in the days of Kievan Rus',

in great and beautiful Kiev. For a thousand years I have
watched over my city—for a time they called me Saint Elias,
but did I not still rule the thunder and cast the lightning?
I am Perun. I am King and god.

Genealogy is a tricky thing. I can trace certain lines of my family back to the 1600s, but no matter what I find out, the same Western European nationalities keep repeating: English, Dutch, Swiss, French, Scottish. I am descended from two *different* families that supported Charles I during the English Civil War and who had to leave the country rather suddenly when Cromwell came to power. (One went to Maryland and one to Grand Cayman, but the outcome was the same.)

So why in the name of all that's holy do I have this insane liking for Slavic deities? As far as I'm concerned, Perun, in a word, *rocks*. I have prayed to him and welcomed him into ritual, and his presence resonates with me. I think it's because Perun is the King archetype in all its powerful glory: nothing held back, nothing restrained. Perun is the King, and he knows it and fills his role admirably.

I find it interesting that Perun and Veles share a kinship even though they are opposites; one cannot exist without the other. In fact, when Slavic Europe was finally Christianized (which took a long time; Lithuania was the last European nation to accept Christianity as a state religion), most of the old myths merely became stories of two saints, or of God and the Devil. Not unlike the traditions of the African diaspora, the Slavs hid their traditional gods in Christian disguises. But no matter what mufti Perun might be wearing, he is the very spirit of determined power.

Often when we deal with our own King, we let our fears circumscribe our desires, dreams, and purposes. Perun is the embodied refutation to that self-limiting tendency. When our King steps forth and declares his desire and his dreams, we must step forward as well—seizing our power and accepting that our desires are part of the natural order of things. We are more often afraid of our own magnificence than our own unworthiness; I know that one of my greatest fears is not of failing but of succeeding. On some level, we all know how great we are and what magnificent gifts we have been given as men; but our fears, our early programming, and societal pressure conspire to keep us from ever realizing these gifts.

The King energy inherent in Perun is our answer to that. We step forward and ride the lightning, accept the blessing of our own power, and admit that frankly we're pretty special in our own right. Every man I see has the potential to be a powerful, magnificent, enlightened man, if only he sees that same power in himself. Enthroned and robed in the King's trappings, we become Kings ourselves.

For Further Thought

Am I capable of just *being* rather than doing? If not, why not?

Can I respond with benevolence to anger and attacks from my King?

What are my dreams and visions? What power do I have to make them come true?

MAGICKAL WORKING

Enthroning the Self

For me at least, the ultimate purpose of magick is self-exploration and self-expression. Everything else is theatre. I do magick because I want to make changes in myself and then see those changes reflected in the world around me.

As such, my style of magick tends to be somewhat internal and self-referential. This ritual is no exception; the ritual of enthroning the self is designed to aid you in stepping fully into your King, and as such to find out what dreams you want to make manifest.

Recommended Tools

- A purple candle. If you can't find purple, go with some other royal color. It should be a candle that will take at most a few hours to burn.

- A knife. You need a knife that feels good in your hand and that you don't mind getting wax on. The Wusthof, for example, is right out.

- A crown. No, I don't mean a literal crown. But some sort of symbol of the primal sign of royalty works wonders. Heck, take your kid to Burger King if you have to.

- A throne. Go for a comfortable, high chair.

- The standard altar.

Set your altar and call the directions (page 262).

Sit in your chair for a moment and consider your inner King. Feel him within yourself—strong, powerful, capable of great visions. If you need to, write down the visions you feel are important, although that's not required. Say to yourself:

I call to my inner King. Show me my power.

Repeat this over and over, quietly, and feel yourself slipping into a trance state. As you do, set the crown on your head or put it nearby where you can see it. You are the King—you know what your great dreams and visions are.

At this point, take the knife and carve symbols into your candle that represent the dreams and visions that you, standing in your full King, want to make manifest. Concentrate on the realities behind those visions. Really invest each symbol with magick and will and intention.

Once you have carved the candle, set it to burning *providing you have the time to burn it completely*. It needs to be burned in one sitting, so save it if you can't let it burn out by yourself at this time.

Close the circle as normal. Sit for a while with your inner King and see if any messages or feelings come through.

RITUAL OF AFFIRMATION

Eldering of the Mature Man

The greatest tragedy *in interpersonal relations*[44] in our current era is the discounting of the mature and the elders in our society. In just over one hundred years, elders —those over, say, fifty—have gone from being respected and honored to being ignored, discounted, dismissed, or stuck in little boxes and visited on Sundays. Sometimes. Maybe.

---

44. I make this clarification because I don't want anyone thinking I'm discounting the Holocaust, or Rwanda, or Darfur, or the Turkish massacre of the Armenians, or 9/11, or any of the other horrors the last century has brought us. Robert Heinlein's characters often referred to this time period as the "Crazy Years." I think he was on to something.

While in an ideal world I'd advocate bringing back the extended family, I'm too much of a realist to think that it would work. However, I know that in my own men's work the influence of elder men—Jimmy N., Ed A. (the man who got me to do the New Warrior Training Adventure weekend in the first place), the late Larry D., Mike F., Joe S., Scott J., and many others—has been the single most important influence in developing my own feelings and direction. The elder male, to me, is the teacher. He is the guardian of spiritual and psychic safety. He is the memory and the will of the tribe. He is the repository of wisdom—his own and others'. Most men don't get that gift, to be given wisdom by an elder man. Frankly, that's a damned shame.

As such, I write this ritual in hope that men will learn to honor their elders and honor the Elder in themselves. While I still occasionally bemoan my current age (sliding headfirst down the slippery slope towards forty), I also look forward to when, at age fifty, I can declare myself an elder in the ManKind Project and begin that phase of my work.

A simple altar should be laid with a God and Goddess candle, quarter candles, and symbols of the elements: a wand, a blade, a cup, and a stone. A wooden or stone bowl should also be available on the altar; each person attending the ritual is encouraged to bring a bead that symbolizes a wish for the elder's future or a memory from his past. (It doesn't hurt, however, to request in the invitation to the eldering ceremony that all the beads have the same drill-hole size.)

As a gesture towards complementary energy, the primary officiant of the ritual is a youth—a young man between, say, eighteen and twenty-five who figures importantly in the Elder candidate's life.

> **Youth:** We welcome you to this place where our brother, [*name*], steps into his eldership and seeks to provide wisdom for others doing the great work. At this time, we would ask our brother to welcome in the directions, energies, and honored ancestors as he sees fit.

> *The Elder candidate calls the directions and welcomes the gods as he wishes.*

> **Youth:** The Elder in our society is vitally needed and tragically ignored. In acknowledging our brother's self-designation as Elder, we acknowledge that he has gifts to give us and that he has been and will continue to be a positive influence on our lives. We acknowledge that he is taking responsibility for the greater safety of his tribe however he sees it: not safety of the body, for that is the provenance of the Warrior, but safety of the soul, the spirit, the psyche.

> At this time, I would like to ask anyone who wishes to do so to step forward and share something about our brother that shows he has been or will be an Elder to them, and to place a bead in the offering bowl.

Story time! No, seriously, this is the time for everyone to share stories about the Elder candidate or to give him wishes and hopes for his upcoming eldership. Take the time; this is a celebration of a life and an honoring of a choice. When everyone has finished, the Youth brings the Elder to the altar.

Youth: It is time. Declare yourself Elder in your own words, however you choose to do so.

The Elder makes his own declaration of eldership, however he sees it.

All Present: So witnessed.

Youth: We welcome you as an Elder, [*name*]. I commend to you the watchword of the King: *manifestation.* May you bring us wisdom and teach us and yourself to make your dearest dreams manifest in the real world.

Close the circle as desired by the new Elder—and celebrate!

XIII

THE HEALER
BODY, SOUL, MIND, AND SPIRIT

Blessed are they who heal you of self-despisings.
Of all services which can be done to man,
I know of none more precious.

—William Hale White

If I had known I was going to live this long, I would
have taken better care of myself.

—Mickey Mantle

Men don't take care of themselves. You don't believe me? Here we go:

- In a 2006 address, Professor Alan White of Britain's Royal College of Nursing noted that "on average, rates of death of young men were over 2.5 times that of young women." Describing the extent to which men ignore their own health issues, Dr. White stated that "the rate of death as a result of cardio-vascular disease and cancer increase three- to four-fold in the 35–44 age group when compared to the 25–34 age group, suggesting that problems have been building up in the years when men are known to be poor at accessing health care or paying serious attention to their own health needs."[45]

- A survey by the Commonwealth Fund, a foundation dedicated to promoting good health, discovered that men were "three times more likely than women to say they hadn't seen a doctor in the previous year. And 27

---

45. "Lifestyle Still Cutting Short Men's Lives," eMaxHealth, www.emaxhealth .com/3/5303.html (accessed September 10, 2007).

  percent of men reported not having a regular doctor despite having health insurance."[46]

- It's not only that men avoid regular health checkups. The Commonwealth Fund survey also found that 24 percent of men stated they would "wait as long as possible before seeing a doctor even if they were sick or in pain."[47]

- A 1998 survey by CNN and *Men's Health* magazine found that a third of American men haven't had a checkup in the past year. Nine million American men hadn't seen a doctor at all during the past five years.[48]

Are you starting to get the picture here? Due to some misplaced machismo, men don't take care of themselves. And because we don't take care of ourselves, we die before our time. That's as blunt and as simple as I can put it.

And I know this from experience. As I write this, I'm extremely overweight, arthritic, and hypertensive . . . yet it's only in the last seven or so years I've taken care of my hypertension, and I'm still coming up with excuses for why I don't exercise regularly. I am living proof that it harms us if we ignore the messages our bodies tell us.

---

46. "Real Men Go to the Doctor," Methodist Health System (Dallas, TX), www .methodisthealthsystem.org/ca/11317.htm (accessed September 10, 2007).

47. Ibid.

48. "Why Don't More Men Go to the Doctor?" *Daily News Bulletin*, Los Alamos National Laboratory (June 19, 1998), www.lanl.gov/orgs/pa/News/061998.html (accessed September 10, 2007).

My father, whom I talked about in chapter IX, didn't really take care of himself—and I lost him when I was twenty-three. I want as few men as possible to have to go through that—including my own kids, who are my only motivation to get out and do something, anything, for my own health.

But why is it not enough for us to do it for ourselves?

As men, we have ambiguous relationships at best with healing, nurturing, and accepting help from others. I suspect the reason is related to something we've discussed before: needing healing and nurturing is perceived as a weakness, and in the highly competitive and combative environment of male society, a weakness can be lethal. To a certain extent, that programming is genetic, but we can certainly do a better job of overcoming it than we do. To accept healing, especially healing from another man, takes effort; to admit we are wounded takes even more. But the early deaths and poor health of men is, in my humble opinion, as much psychology as physiology. If heart attacks strike us, it may be as much a result of stress and suppressed sorrow as hardened arteries and a poor diet.

The Tale of Chiron

Chiron was the child of the titan Kronos and the nymph Philyra, engendered while Philyra was trying to escape from the pursuit of Kronos in mare form; Kronos took on stallion form during the encounter. When Chiron was born, he was half god and half horse, the first centaur, and was rejected by his mother and left to wander the world alone.

Eventually, Chiron was adopted by Apollo, the god of the sun, healing, music, and prophecy. Apollo taught Chiron all his knowledge, and Chiron became the immortal guide and guardian to Jason (of the Argonauts), Achilles, and Aesclepius, who became the Hellenic god of medicine.

Sadly, though, Chiron was wounded by an accident with an arrow fired by Heracles. Heracles had tipped his arrows with the blood of the Hydra, which meant the wound would never heal and Chiron would remain in terrible pain until he died. Unfortunately, Chiron, being immortal, would not die.

The centaur soldiered on in pain for a very long time, providing his wisdom and healing to others. In time, though, Heracles begged the gods to free his friend and teacher from his pain. Zeus agreed that Chiron could take the place of Prometheus, who was chained to a rock for offenses against the gods. When Chiron was chained to the rock, he was no longer immortal—and in that moment he died and passed into the starry firmament to become a constellation.

Right now I find that my life in reference to writing this book is a long, complicated exercise in synchronicity. The same day I began this section on the Healer, I watched the premiere of the second season of the TV show *Criminal Minds*—which referred frequently to the concept of scarring after mental trauma and healing wounds—and I attended a ManKind Project Head, Heart, and Soul presentation. Head, Heart, and Soul is the introductory presentation for those interested in the New Warrior Training Adventure; its central theme is that modern life causes layers of scarring and defenses for men that mean we lose touch with our Golden Child, our inner joy and trusting soul.

Chiron is the Wounded Healer. Wounded Healers have suffered some terrible injury, usually through betrayal or negligence, and have learned to function despite the pain. The pain never goes away, though, and the Wounded Healer perpetually lives with that pain—with scar tissue that doesn't quite stretch the way it should—and the memory of the betrayal.

There are very few men who are not Wounded Healers.

Chiron exemplifies every man who has ever taken a wound but kept moving. We all take wounds—often with men it's very early in our childhood, the first time we realize that the unconditional love we get as infants starts to develop conditions and strings as we get older. We are asked to behave in certain ways, fit certain patterns, and are told—either literally or inferentially—that our continued love depends on it. We are told we're not good enough. We don't meet our parents'—and especially our fathers'—expectations. We are wounded, and we develop the defenses to protect ourselves from the world.

Those defenses take a lot of forms: anger, fear, addictions, desires. What Chiron teaches us is that we can step past those defenses and still reach out into the world. The fact is this: nothing can make us forget our wounds. There is no handy water of Lethe. Chiron challenges us to step past our wounds and to reach out to others with the energy and blessing of our Golden Child. Through that stepping forward we can be healed in both body and mind—perhaps not perfect, but certainly able and willing.

Is it easy? No. In the immortal words of Annie Savoy: "The world is made for people who aren't cursed with self-awareness."[49] But it is only through self-awareness that we can be fully functional and fully alive, and being aware of the pain and the damage from our wounds is part of the process. We've seen that men don't like to take care of their physical health; they're even worse, in my humble opinion, at taking care of their emotional health. We're afraid of even seeing our wounds, much less dealing with them.

That's why group men's work is so important. In group work we can support each other and develop our own compensations for our wounds. Together we too can become healers of each other and of the world.

The Tale of Baldur

I am fair of feature, and so bright light shines from me. I am the wisest of the Aesir, the most gracious and gentle, and I am fair-spoken so that all who hear my words hearken to them. I am the peaceful center of a clan of warriors, the son who brings peace to the family. I am the master of Breidablik; in that place, my home, nothing unclean can exist, and all is fresh, new, and shining with power and light. I am the soul of summer.

Do you know me? I am the second son of Odin. My wife is Nanna, my son Forseti. I bring light and joy and

---

49. *Bull Durham*, DVD, directed by Ron Shelton (1988; Los Angeles: MGM Home Entertainment).

simple mirth to the Aesir. I know the science of runes;
I am a master of herbs and simples, and chamomile is
"Baldur's brow." My judgments are firm and wise, and
my son Forseti is the conciliator of all disputes and the
moderator of disagreements, even between the gods.

I am the lord of the summer sunlight, and the dark-
ening of my brow shall bring winter, and then summer
again.

This section may result in an angry horde of Ásatrú on my front lawn.

I am aware that in orthodox and traditional reading of Norse myth there is no particular support for calling Baldur a healing deity. However, I'm going to go out on a limb here and say that he is. Look at the symbols used: light, purity, justice, mediation, herbs and simples . . . if Baldur isn't a healer, I'm not sure I'd recognize a healer if it bit me on the edda.

To me at least, Baldur is the personification of the healing of the spirit and of purification. Like the sauna that arose in his part of the world, he removes poisons not only from the body but also from the soul. There is no darkness or impurity in him; he is the open arms and fully accepting joy and peace that comes from a true healing of the spirit. In many ways, Baldur *is* the Golden Child, reaching out to us from behind our defenses and encouraging us to come bask in the summer sun.

Men submit themselves to astonishing levels of spiritual toxicity. We go out into the world and voluntarily submit ourselves to other people's negative emotions every day, and we rarely even think about it—much less do anything about it. Most men no longer have the sweat lodge or vision quest or spiritual retreat or meditation circle to concentrate on removing the taint of the negativity we are immersed in constantly. If on the one hand we don't deal with our own anger and sorrow—which we've seen pretty clearly—and on the other hand we don't deal with the anger and sorrow of others that we're surrounded by, then how long before we drown in it all? How long before it kills us?

Baldur reminds us in his equal-handed joy and simplicity to stop every so often, clean ourselves up, and experience the world in all its radiance. How you clean up is your own business—whether it's a weekend retreat, a sweat lodge, church, coven, I-Group, or racquetball game, it must be done, and I know that if I don't take the time to do it bad things happen.

Spiritual toxicity is especially lethal to a man who calls himself a healer. It can build up until it all explodes and we make poor choices.

The Tale of Dian Cecht and Miach

Now when the Tuatha Dé Danann came to Ireland, they were met by the Fir Bolg, who held that land and were determined to keep it. In that battle, the battle of Magh Tuiredh, Nuada, the leader of the Dé Danann, lost his hand. A rightful king could not be imperfect in body, so a solution had to be found.

The healer of the Dé Danann, Dian Cecht, fashioned himself a hand of silver, cunningly jointed and fully movable, and did gift it to Nuada, and it was a wonder to behold. But Miach, the son of Dian Cecht, thought to himself that this was not good enough for the king,

*and so he betook himself to heal Nuada. Three days did
Miach hold Nuada's hand against his side and three days
against his breast, and Nuada was fully healed.*

*Dian Cecht was jealous of his son's healing of the
king, and besides did not approve of the methods Miach
used. So he smote him upon the head three times, and each
time did Miach heal himself from his father's blows—but
the fourth blow destroyed Miach's brain and that even he
could not heal. So Miach died.*

*On dying, Miach turned into three hundred and
sixty-five herbs with great magickal and medicinal powers. His sister Airmed took those herbs in her apron and
separated them by type and use so that they could be best
used for healing. But Dian Cecht took her apron and
shook it, scattering the herbs so that no man could know
all the herb lore.*

Well. What in the heck is *this* about?

On the surface, the myth of Dian Cecht and Miach
seems to be confusing at best. It gets even worse when you
realize Dian Cecht's murder of Miach means that Nuada is
no longer truly healed, which means he can't be king, which
drags the war with the Fir Bolg on longer than it should have
gone. Dian Cecht is the healer of the Dé Danann—what in
the heck was he *thinking*?

That's the point. He wasn't.

There are many interpretations of the myth of Dian
Cecht, most of them performed by Celtic pagan scholars who
have much more education than I do. (Some of them even
speak Irish, which to me proves that miracles are possible.)

However, in the context of the work we are doing together in this book, I have my own small bit of wisdom to throw out there. It seems to me that Dian Cecht is acting out of his own wound, the Wounded Healer turning to the ultimate darkness of which he is capable.

Healers work hard. But when a healer goes bad—when his ego or his anger gets in his way—we end up with something terrible. Everyone has heard or seen stories about the heartless, egotistical physician who treats his patients as objects and his colleagues as people to undermine and stab in the back. Because I believe that human beings are not inherently evil (save in cases of organic dysfunction such as psychopathy), I assume that this behavior comes out of some sort of deep wound. The fact remains, however, that the behavior is there. When a healer gets lost in his ego, he becomes dangerous. In Dian Cecht's case, he even suppresses knowledge—perhaps because he fears that if humans gain true herb lore, he won't be needed any more. Similarities between this and the doctor who talks down to patients—or tells them nothing at all—are hard to avoid.

So how do we as men avoid this pitfall?

Once again, we have to trust other men to help us keep control of our egos and stay out of shadow. My shadow can be a raging egotist; I don't trust anyone else to do anything because, frankly, they'll just fuck it up. I am the only person I can trust. I am the only person capable. And when I'm in that mindset, other people are less than human. The worst part of all of this may be that I cannot recognize when I'm that far in shadow. It's as if I put on a pair of trick spectacles;

suddenly all the darkness that surrounds me seems good and right and exactly where I'm supposed to be. It seems normal to be that kind of raging egotist. It seems right to be hurting other people because they're incompetent morons.

We've talked about this state of mind before, when we discussed the Warrior. The Warrior gets out of balance when his ego and desires become paramount and people become objects, less than human. The Healer is subject to the exact same weakness and its consequence. The only way to get around that is to keep the ego in check with whatever means seem good to you—but the best way I've found is to listen to others and accept their help. It is only through acknowledging our interconnectedness and dependence on others that I avoid that particular pitfall.

For Further Thought

Am I taking care of myself?

> Am I letting my inner healer out to help others?
>
> Am I discharging the spiritual toxicity I take on?

MAGICKAL WORKING

Finding the Deep Wound

I want to make something very clear before we go any further with this working: I am presenting this piece of magick as an option *only if you have a men's group to work with.* Frankly, I'm uncomfortable with someone doing this working alone.

Also, *if you have been a victim of sexual or physical abuse or other serious childhood traumas, do not do this working!* I can't state that one loudly or emphatically enough. Get a therapist or a psychiatrist to help you analyze the shape of your inner wound. That's why they take on all those student loans; they're trained to do that stuff.

If at any time you feel unsafe or out of control, stop the meditation immediately.

With that said:

This is a guided meditation. As such, it is merely to be read in a comfortable place. While a paper and writing instrument might be useful to take notes, they're not necessary. All pauses in the meditation are designed to be times when you sit, collect your thoughts, and keep yourself centered so that you can continue.

Relax. Let your body go limp and begin breathing slow and easy.

Tense your toes, each one . . . then relax them, toe by toe. Feel the tension wash away. Tense your feet and ankles; feel your skin stretch over the bone, then relax them. Again, feel the tension wash away.

Tense your calf muscles, feeling them knot tightly; then relax them. Tense your knees, then relax them. Tense your thigh muscles, cords moving under your skin—then relax them. Feel your legs lying free, relaxed, light, easy.

Tense your hips. As you do so, feel the energy that lays curled under your testicles and penis stir slowly. Relax your hips, feeling that energy spread out in a slow, calm pool.

Tense your belly. Feel the energy there and relax as before, letting it spread into a smooth, warm pool.

Tense your hands. Feel where the energy flows in and out of your body through your fingers—and then relax, letting your fingers lie limp.

Tense your lower arms and elbows, and relax them. Do the same with your upper arms. Feel your arms lie calm and limp against the chair.

Tense your chest. Feel the energy and weight that lies beneath and above your heart, the burden of a man. Let that burden float away, and the energy smooth out and pool. Relax.

Tense your neck and shoulders. Feel the lines of tension that are always there, the tension that comes from living in today's world with today's pressures. Let your neck and shoulders relax, laying your head back in your chair.

Tense your brow and facial muscles. Let the energy that rests behind your third eye pool and spread throughout your face. Then, finally, feel that pooled energy well out of the crown of your head, embracing you, covering you with relaxing warmth. You are centered and relaxed and calm, ready to work.

First, feel anger. Feel a time when you were aroused, furious, when pure anger filled you. Feel that emotion as well.

(*pause*)

Feel shame. Feel a time when you burned with embarrassment, when you were mortified and wanted to sink through the floor. Meditate on that emotion.

(*pause*)

Feel sadness. Feel a time when you mourned, when something precious was taken from you. Meditate on that emotion.

(*pause*)

Finally, feel fear. Feel a time when you were terrified, when the world was a threatening place. Meditate on that emotion.

(*pause*)

Each of these emotions can come from a deep wound in your childhood. The emotional patterns we evoke and use throughout our lives are programmed early. Ask yourself now: which emotion felt strongest to you?

Once you find that strongest emotion, go back in your memories. Find the earliest time in your life you felt that emotion. What was happening? Ask yourself if that memory is where you learned to feel that emotion, and ask yourself if that incident has programmed how you respond to the world today.

If it is so, journal the incident if you desire. When you feel that emotion in your daily life, ask yourself if you are truly responding to the situation you are currently in or if you are responding based on your deep wound.

Now, feel joy. Feel the happiest moment of your life, the most exhilarating and transcendent experience you have ever had. Allow yourself time to feel that joy, and then take it into yourself. Let it be your refuge when your other emotions overwhelm you.

(*pause*)

Once you have finished the meditation and identified this issue, ground, relax, and step out of that space. Be aware of your current surroundings; be aware of who you currently are, how old you are, where you are in the moment. When you are fully aware and out of that altered state, do any more journaling you want to do.

RITUAL OF AFFIRMATION

Blessing of a Men's Group

In 1992, I was hanging out with a bunch of friends who were all interested in Wicca. The problem was that I was living in Indianapolis where there were no public and eclectic covens. There were a couple of group options, but none of them were open—and they certainly wouldn't take a group at once.

So, armed only with battered copies of Cunningham and Starhawk, this valiant band of twenty-somethings who should have known better started their own coven. We made a lot of mistakes. We stumbled through a lot of drama. But that same coven, now under the care of my longtime close friends and students Avatar and Kat, still exists more than fifteen years later.

Needless to say, I'm a big fan of forming your own group when there's no other option available. In that spirit, I offer this ritual.

The group of men seeking to form a men's circle should determine a man to lead this ritual—he will be the Speaker for the circle. There should be an altar set with quarter candles, God and Goddess candles, and symbols of the elements. On, next to, or near the altar there should be a box—while a fine wooden chest would be cool, there is nothing wrong with a Rubbermaid™ container if that's what you have. Finally, there should be some sort of large crystal or stone to use as the group's heartstone.

Each man should be asked to bring a sacred object to donate to the group. These could include books, smudge, a rattle[50] and smudge pot for smudging, a staff for a talking stick and for calling direction, an ablutions bowl for cleansing, divination tools, stones, god or goddess figures, or whatever else seems good to the man in question. What is important to bear in mind is that each man have something, and each man have an intention or purpose around that object.

Finally, the group will need a name before this ritual is performed. That doesn't mean the name can't change later, but there needs to be a statement of intention—a naming, to paraphrase Madeleine L'Engle—that fixes the energy and purpose of the group.

> **Speaker:** We are gathered here to create a group that is greater than the sum of its parts.
>
> Spirit of the East, essence of Air, bring us wisdom and bless our undertaking here.
>
> Spirit of the South, essence of Fire, bring us enthusiasm and bless our undertaking here.
>
> Spirit of the West, essence of Water, bring us empathy and bless our undertaking here.
>
> Spirit of the North, essence of Earth, bring us grounding and bless our undertaking here.
>
> **Men:** So mote it be!
>
> **Speaker:** Great Goddess, eternal other half of our manhood, we ask your blessing here tonight. May we always treat women as nobly as we want ourselves to be treated. So mote it be!

---

50. Many spiritual traditions use a rattle while people are being smudged as a meditative source of "white noise."

Great God, eternal spirit of our manhood, we ask your blessing here tonight. May we grow in your spirit to become better men, better brothers, and better humans. So mote it be!

Speaker: We gather here to form a community of men.

We will as a community support each other rather than tear each other down.

We will as a community care for each other instead of harming each other.

We will as a community tell the truth to each other rather than lie.

We will as a community challenge each other rather than allowing each other to exist in shadow.

We will as a community live our lives in service to the greater community, fulfilling our life's mission with support from our brothers.

Now, I ask each man to step forward and offer something to the community, and speak to why his gift was chosen and what he needs from and offers to this group.

At this time, each man steps forward, offers his gift, and speaks his truth. As he speaks, he lays a hand on the heartstone of the group or holds it, putting that energy into the stone.

Speaker: Each man here has spoken to his needs and his gifts. If there is a man here who is not willing to support his brothers, to tell them the truth, to support them, challenge them, cry with them, laugh with them, and watch their backs, leave now.

This assumes no men leave, naturally. The Speaker holds the heartstone.

Now let it be said at this time in this place that [*name*], a circle of men, is created. I commend to you the watchword of the Healer: *sustaining*. May we also sustain great works in this company. So mote it be!

Assembled Men: So mote it be!

Allow the ceremony to degenerate into hugging and tom-foolery for a bit.

Speaker: The Earth of determination, the Water of love, the Fire of the spirit, and the Air of wisdom; we thank and bless their spirits, knowing they are with us always.

We thank the Great Goddess, She who is our other soul, for standing with us tonight. We thank the Great God, He who is our root and our spirit, for standing with us tonight. We go now and begin our journey.

XIV

THE SACRIFICED ONE

THE END AND THE BEGINNING

Cattle die, kinsmen die
the self must also die;
I know one thing which never dies:
the reputation of each dead man.

—*The Hávamál,* Strophe 77

This chapter is last for a reason.

Bluntly put, this is the archetype that is likely to have the most charge from a societal viewpoint. Whether someone is personally a Pagan, Christian, Jew, Muslim, Baha'i, Unitarian, or whatever, the simple truth is that if one is talking about the archetype of the Sacrificed One, then one has to deal with Christ. To ignore that is like ignoring the pink elephant in your living room—you can do it, but eventually someone's going to have to deal with the fact that the living room is 80 percent occupied and slowly being covered in pachyderm poop.

So I'll charge blindly forward and start it off with these two seemingly contradictory statements:

- There are very few people who can mix Christian and Pagan practice and beliefs successfully;[51]

- Nevertheless, I think Christ as Sacrificed One is a valid and powerful archetype that people of many faiths can learn from.

---

51. Though my coven and ManKind Project brother Silverwolf can pull it off and make it look easy. If you think that a Wiccan priest can't invoke Michael the Archangel, you're a little short-sighted.

We should probably discuss our terms first. Who is the Sacrificed One? Easy: it is the figure whose death and resurrection is a necessary trigger for something to happen to keep the world running. That outcome can be salvation, spring, or wisdom, but there has to be a death and a return, and it has to be an essential death and rebirth, without which something good doesn't happen.

The key word here is *necessary*. While that may sound a lot like the sacrifice of the Lover from chapter IV, the motivation is different somehow. That's not to say the Sacrificed One doesn't love—indeed, he does, to the point of his own death—but there is a greater cosmic sense of purpose that overlays it. The Lover chooses to sacrifice himself; the Sacrificed One is, in many ways, born to it and cannot escape it although he might want to. (Witness the myth of Gethsemane.)

I read a lot, and I admit that I get a little weepy at books. The one scene I'm guaranteed to get all choked up over is the death of Prince Diarmuid dan Ailell toward the end of Guy Gavriel Kay's *The Fionavar Tapestry*. Diarmuid rides forth at sunset and breaks a cycle of incarnation and pain for Arthur, Guinevere, and Lancelot, dying in the process in the arms of his beloved, carried into death by the dagger of his brother so that he is not killed at the hands of evil. He defeats the darkness, but it costs him his life. It is a great deed—perhaps the greatest. But dammit, I still cry. The Sacrificed One's hallmark is tears, even as we know that the sacrifice is necessary and for the greater good.

The Tale of the Christ

Once upon a time there was a special little boy. He was born in a cave, in spring, because the ruler had asked everyone to return to their hometown to be counted and there was no room at the inn. For company the baby boy had animals and the shepherds who had come there, perhaps guided by Spirit or a bright star, as they had been in the fields guarding the new lambs.

The boy grew up. He was a very bright boy, and eventually he found his purpose and asked another man to initiate him into his mission. His mission was simple: to convince people that perhaps it would be a good idea to stop hurting each other, and to explain to them that salvation and enlightenment didn't come from being in the right tribe or the right cult, but rather from understanding that he was the Son of God—and so was everyone else, if they would only see it.

Many people heard his message. Some believed it. Some didn't. When he took on his Warrior aspect and cleared thieves and petty merchants out of his people's holy place, he made enemies. When he took on his Healer aspect and raised the dead, or stepped into his Magician and cast out madness, some were afraid. When in service to his own inner King he refused to be called the king of his tribe and overthrow the foreigners, he made more enemies. And finally the authorities came to get him. He could have refused, recanted, accepted the offer of a foreign judge who was trying to help him escape his fate—but had he done that, would he be living his mission anymore? Or if he dealt with his death without fear, would that sacrifice mean that death would become something less to fear for everyone else?

So he was killed, willingly. Many say he came back. His spirit certainly did, and even though an ugly little man followed him and wrote letters about misogyny and anger and other men have done horrible things in his name—things that he would not have countenanced—the fact remains that the door he opened remains open, regardless of tribe.

There's a lot that can be said here, and most of it has been beaten like a dead horse. There are, however, some things that just don't make sense on an initial reading.

In the myth of the trial and crucifixion, we have the rather ambiguous figure of Pilate. It's pretty obvious, no matter what interpretation of the story you read, that Pilate didn't want to have Christ killed. He was looking for any possible loophole to get out of having to kill someone he considered slightly dotty but not a bad sort. So why did it happen?

That's easy. Christ refused to back down on his principles, no matter how many ways out Pilate tried to provide. We have seen throughout history that if you have principles and you stick to them—loudly if necessary—you run the risk of getting yourself killed. Gandhi, King, Hypatia, Joe Hill, Matthew Shepard, Titus Brandsma, Anna Mae Aquash—the list is entirely too long and too bloody. And every time we stand up to fight injustice, the fact remains that we may very well have to deal with that ourselves.

In ten years and more of Pagan activism, I have never had to face death myself. But I also have dealt with physical threats made against Pagan Pride volunteers, people losing children and jobs, and even the death of Tempest Smith. To be a principled man and to have the desire to change the world can make you a target. That's part of what we can learn from Christ: we may be a target, and it doesn't matter. For us to remain in integrity with ourselves—to achieve our life's mission—we have to stand our ground, even if that results in negative consequences. Even if the Sacrificed One is offered an out, a way to have the cup of bitterness pass from his lips, he cannot take it and still achieve his goal.

Sacrifice can take many forms; thankfully, crucifixion is out of fashion and we may never have to give our lives for our beliefs. But the Sacrificed One teaches us that if we do, we must do it with integrity and surety. If the Sacrifice is asked for, it must be, in the end, done with an open and accepting heart.

The Tale of Prometheus

Are you warm? Do you breathe? Do you feel? Then thank me, man, should you consider it worth it.

I am Prometheus, the son of Iapetos. My first cousin, Zeus, is the ruler of the Olympian gods of Greece—but I created man out of base clay and water, and begged soul for them from Athena. My brother Epimetheus, who created animals, gave them speed and strength and tooth and claw—all I had was soul, but I gave that willingly. I even grew fond of my creations, and wanted them to grow and develop.

I asked Zeus to give mankind fire. He refused, think-ing men would be powerful and arrogant if given that great gift. (Perhaps he also feared they would be like the gods.) But I stole fire from his lightning and gave it to man. I also tricked him, when he was discussing the proper forms of sacrifice to the gods, to take the skin and organs and bones and leave man the meat.

I did all this for man. Yet in the end my deeds caught up to me and Zeus chained me to a rock. He sent an eagle, one of his sacred birds, to tear into me and eat my liver every day—and because I am immortal, it re-grew over-night and each day I suffered new pain.

In time I was freed, and I rose again to take my place on Mount Olympus. But I have never forgotten my sacri-fice for man. Indeed, it was worth it to see fire in man's camps and in his eyes.

I recall as a child being truly grossed out by the myth of Pro-metheus. The whole concept of having one's liver eternally consumed by a bird, day after day, was just . . . I don't know, really unspeakable to me as an eight-year-old.

As an adult, I don't think it's much better. Prometheus is punished most viciously for—again—remaining loyal to his principles. He believes humans deserves more, and he defies Zeus. This is generally considered an unwise move in Hel-lenic myth, as Zeus tends to be rather insistent in getting his own way.

Prometheus brings us fire. In our own lives, we often have to sacrifice to bring others fire—be it the fire of passion, belief, self-knowledge, or wisdom. One of the things that usually surprises the men who go through the New Warrior Training Adventure is that staff members pay to be there. We don't get a free ride—we pay and we give up work.

That's an incredibly small example in a cosmic sense, but it exemplifies what we're talking about. Whether it's an NWTA weekend, Dr. Tom Dooley in the Indochinese jungle, or Prometheus on his rock, it takes sacrifice to bring fire to others.

We've talked about having a life mission before. Missions can often be boiled down to bringing some sort of additional fire and light to the world. My mission is about education. Another man's may be about creativity, or passion, or leadership. As men, we're often afraid to bring that kind of passion and mission into play. Our society has taught us not to stick our heads out or stand out from the crowd, or we'll get hammered down like a Whac-A-Mole at Chuck E. Cheese's.

Part of being fully masculine and fully alive is to meet that learned behavior—the programming to keep our heads down—with courage and purpose and mission. Prometheus suffered, yes—as we saw in the tale of Chiron, he did eventually get out, but he hurt an awful lot before he did so. We may never be chained to a rock, but we can be chained to other people's prejudices toward us. And as men we are more likely to be active, kinetic, willing to meet those challenges and prejudices head on. It's one of the ways we can take that hard-wired desire for conflict and channel it into something constructive and world-healing.

The question then becomes: is bringing others that fire worth it? My unshakable opinion is that it is. The world will never change until we change it, one person at a time, one thing at a time, one fire at a time. Prometheus saw the greatness in us as humans that spurred him on to take the risk he took. In the final summation, we sell ourselves short if we don't do the same.

The Tale of John Barleycorn

I am John Barleycorn and I must die.

I am the lord of the grain and the spirit of the grain. I am planted in the spring, and I raise my head higher in the sunlight and the rain. At summer's height, I reach for the sky, with my swelling seeds and strong stalk.

But even then, I know I must die.

Late summer will come, and early fall, and I will turn from green to gold. And in time men will come with scythes and cut me down. I will fall, I will bleed, and I will die.

The miller will take my seed and grind it, and the baker will bake it, and the brewer will make good beer with it, and men will be happy and fed.

And a few seeds will fall as I die.

And they will sprout come spring, and men will sow more seeds with them.

And I will return as I always do, and once again lift my face to the sun.

Because I must die . . .

And I must return.

The cycle of growth, death, and rebirth is really the axiomatic source of the Sacrificed One. Nothing is sacrificed so much as the seasons themselves; it is no wonder that almost all myth cycles have some explanation of the turning of the seasons.

John Barleycorn's tale has a lot of roots (no agricultural pun intended, really). It may come from the Welsh myth of Llew and Goronwy, and it can definitely be seen reflected in the Traditionalist Wicca tale of the Oak King and the Holly King. In both cases, a sun deity rules for six months of the year and is then overthrown by a dark lord, who also rules for six months.

But in this case I think it's best to just look at it without any additional interpretations, as the heart of all Sacrifice tales.

It is an unavoidable truth in nature that things die so that other things can live. There's a big food chain, and everything and everyone has its place on it. John Barleycorn is a living manifestation of the cycle of birth and death and rebirth personified as the god of the grain, and as such he reminds us that we, too, have our place in the circle of life. We are born, we will die, and our atoms will return to the pool of energy and be eventually reborn as something else. Our souls, too, are reborn into another life. Just as the grain is harvested and turned into nourishment, so too are we harvested in our time and taken to another life, another incarnation, another learning experience.

This is the lesson of John Barleycorn—that nothing really dies and nothing is ever lost. We are men standing on the shoulders of our ancestors, with the generations stretching out ahead of us. What we do now to reclaim the sacred masculine is vitally important, because that cycle will continue independently of our existence this time around. We will shape the future, and then we will be the future when the wheel of karma rolls around again.

We spend a lot of time outrunning the cycle of life. Men in particular seem to think that the natural progression through the stages of life is our enemy; we've talked about midlife crises and being children past our time. When it comes down to it, we don't grow old gracefully and we fear death. John Barleycorn and the Sacrificed One teach us that in the end we will all die and we will all return, and the great work of masculinity will continue.

For Further Thought

Have you backed down from your principles, or are you still standing strong?

Have you brought anyone fire? Do you need someone to bring *you* fire?

Are you afraid of the cycle of life, or are you content with your place in it?

MAGICKAL WORKING

Giving Up

This is what you do when you can't do anything else.

Every man has been in this situation. You've put your heart, soul, lifeblood, time, and energy into a situation—and it's just not working. You can't stick with the situation anymore; you have to get out and move on. You have to have your own life again.

Our society's definition of masculinity says that we have to stay by our post, we have to stick with it. But the Sacrificed One teaches us that sometimes things have to end for them to begin. It is in that spirit that this working is presented.

Recommended Tools

- Yarn. Pick a color that resonates with the issue you need freedom from: red for a love affair, green for bad business matters, and so forth.

- A pair of scissors.

- An object that represents you. It does need to be solid enough to wrap yarn around, so a photo probably won't work.

- A black candle.

For starters, this is a banishing ritual, so everything is done backwards. The circle is cast counterclockwise (also known as antisunwise or widdershins, depending on your magickal tradition) and the energy is visualized as counterclockwise. However, the yarn is wrapped around the representative object *clockwise*. This is important.

Cast the circle and call the directions (page 262). Hold the representative object up. Say:

This is my life, this is who I want to be.
　　Great god, Sacrificed One, opener of the way,
　　Help me to free myself from the situation I am in.
　　Help me to be liberated from the chains that bind me.
　　So mote it be!

Light the black candle. Take the yarn and begin to wrap the representative object in it, slowly and thoughtfully. Bear in mind the chains that you have wrapped around you, the decisions you have made that you need to be freed from. Do this act mindfully, accepting responsibility for the choices you have made but asking to be free of them now.

Hold up the now-cocooned object and consider it for a long moment.

This is my life; I want to be free from this.
> *Great God, sacrificed one, I accept my own responsibility in this action.*
> *Free me from the chains I am entombed in*
> *But keep me in integrity with my own actions.*
> *So mote it be!*

Take the scissors and carefully cut the wrapped yarn away from the figure. Cut it, if possible, in one even stroke or set of strokes. Make the cut with clean intention, and remove the limitations you have accepted on yourself.

I wish to be free.
> *I wish to be in my own life again.*
> *Great God, bless me in this undertaking.*

Place the representative object on the altar and consider it for a while. When you are ready, close the circle. Dispose of the yarn—burial is best.

Ritual of Affirmation

A Men's Healing Circle

I spent a lot of time wondering to myself whether or not this should actually be in the Healer chapter rather than here. I finally decided on this placement because a healing circle is, at least to me, a door between two worlds, that of the active and the infirm—and the Sacrificed One guards that door.

So without further ado:

Men who attend this ritual should bring a drum if possible. They should also bring a small sacred object of some sort for a healing bundle they will make. Smudge is passed around the circle before the ritual begins to cleanse and renew the men involved.

The altar is simple: four quarters, a God and Goddess candle, and symbols of the elements. It should be in the center of the circle. The Elder leads the ritual and speaks all the parts in italics below.

> **Youth:** We welcome the East, the element of Air. The East supports and cleanses and brings the morning's light. Hail and welcome, spirits of the East!

> **Warrior:** We welcome the South, the element of Fire. The South burns away impurities and illness, leaving us tempered and strong. Hail and welcome, spirits of the South!

> **King:** We welcome the West, the element of Water. The West heals and supports, easing the pain of soul as well as body. Hail and welcome, spirits of the West!

Elder: We welcome the North, the element of Earth. The earth grounds and supports and nurtures, bringing us back to health. Hail and welcome, spirits of the North!

Youth: We welcome the Great Goddess, Mother of us all, healer and nurturer.

King: We welcome the Great God, Father of us all, guard and guide.

The Elder steps forward, holding a small cloth, leather, or other bag to use as a healing bundle. As he speaks, he walks deosil (sunwise or clockwise) around the circle.

We gather here to bring healing to our brother [name]. He has asked us for our energy and prayers in this, his time of trial.

I ask that this energy be for the best possible outcome for our brother. If he needs healing of the body, soul, mind, or spirit; if he needs to ease his path towards his destination; or if he just needs to know that we are with him, let this be so. Brothers, I ask you now to put your sacred gift in our brother's healing bundle.

At this time, the Elder passes the bundle around the circle. Men put their gift in the bundle silently, pausing only to hold it for a moment and put their energy into it. Once the bundle has passed back to the Elder and he has placed it on the altar, he begins a slow, heartbeat drumming on his drum. Others join in.

The Elder sets the pace for the drumming. The eventual point is to build energy by gradually increasing tone and tempo and bringing the drumming to a powerful, raucous climax.

When the drumming is done, silence is kept for a bit while the men ground and come back to earth. At this point, a cup of blessed water or juice should be passed, as well as a loaf of bread or some other food. This is vitally important in order to bring the men back to the "now."

When the Elder judges it time, he stands.

We have put energy in this bundle for our brother [name]. Let it bring him healing and renewal for the greater good and for his good.

> *The Earth of determination, the Water of love, the Fire of the spirit, and the Air of wisdom; we thank and bless their spirits, knowing they are with us always. We thank the Great Goddess, She who is our other soul, for standing with us tonight. We thank the Great God, He who is our root and our spirit, for standing with us tonight. We go now and begin our journey.*

The circle then breaks up, each man holding the healing energy in mind as he thinks of the circle's beneficiary. It may be good for the men to stay together for a while.

XV

AFTERWORD
THE ROAD FROM HERE

Every day you may make progress. Every step may be fruitful. Yet there will stretch out before you an ever-lengthening, ever-ascending, ever-improving path. You know you will never get to the end of the journey. But this, so far from discouraging, only adds to the joy and glory of the climb.

—Sir Winston Churchill

Well. Now where to from here?

Sacred Paths for Modern Men is, in the end, a map—and only a partial map at that. The territory of the sacred masculine and the mature masculine is, in the long run, mostly unmapped; we have a great deal of work left to do to heal the wounds and bridge the gaps that keep us from seeing each other as only people—not men or women, not Pagan or Christian or Jewish or Muslim, black or white or Asian or Native, American or European or African. It serves very many people to keep us apart; to come together will be a long struggle.

But we have made a beginning, in so many places. This is just one such beginning, and a rather small one at that. My hope is that somewhere, to someone or more than one someone, this book is useful. My work with Pagan Pride International has been dedicated to changing one mind at a time, and the ManKind Project's motto is "changing the world one man at a time"—so I want one reader at a time to find some wisdom in this belief.

I am, in the end, no different from anyone else. I have no pedigree, lineage, or college degree that says I have permission to discuss Jung as if I know what I'm talking about. I have some common sense, and some experiences. But most of all, what I've had are teachers. From my great-grandfather to my father to my magickal teachers to the men I have worked with to my children, these have been my teachers. If I know anything, it's because I shut up and listened—perhaps not as often as I should have, but I did do it occasionally. This map, this work, is the result.

If you received some wisdom from it, I ask you to pass it on. No, I don't mean ask other people to buy the book (though, admittedly, that would be nice)—I mean be willing to teach and to learn. Be willing to point out the portions of the map that worked for you. Be willing to take chances and reach out to help others.

In the end, a map is only as good as the cartographer. In the frontier of the human spirit and the Sacred, we are all cartographers, scouts, pioneers heading out into an unknown future. We are all, to quote Beagle again, the colonizers of dreams. There may be no greater gift than to sketch the horizon for those around us and those who come after us, so that they may lift their eyes from the darkness around them and the chains on their feet and see that somewhere, somehow, there is a better country, a country of love and equality and joy. Let us go forth together, and find the road back to ourselves. It is, in the end, the adventure that may redeem us.

APPENDIX I
RECIPES, PRAYERS, AND RITUALS

A BASIC CENTERING MEDITATION:
THE ATLAS MEDITATION

You are a man.

Sit quietly, your legs under your body. Hold out your arms, so that you are cradling something above you, a great weight on your shoulders. This weight is your world; as Atlas the titan in Hellenic mythology stood, back bowed, face pained, carrying the world, so too do you, right now, carry the pain and the worry of your world. Feel the weight. Feel the shadow of that weight, those daily concerns and worries, casts upon your heart.

Breathe deeply, and feel that weight shift on your shoulders. It is a heavy thing, isn't it? It crushes your shoulders and your neck and your back and your balls; it keeps you pinned like a butterfly on a collector's card. You are a man; you have to carry the world. That's your job.

But doesn't it make you angry?

Feel the anger begin to burn in your heart. Keep breathing. Do not let the anger overmaster you, but feel that fire burning at the base of your spine. That is the sacred fire, the kundalini, the fire of your bones and blood and balls.

Slowly, breathing easily, with each exhale feel the fire suffuse your form. Feel its heat come down your thighs and legs to your feet. Feel the fire arch up your spine, creeping slowly through belly and heart—and as the fire creeps upward, the fire of your power, feel the weight of the world on your shoulders lighten. Feel Atlas finally begin to stretch, and you yourself stretch, sitting up, arching your back so that you are free, not pinned, not crushed.

Feel the fire move upward through your heart, freeing the knot of stress that you may find there. Feel it move through your voice, so that you can roar like a wild man, sing like a bard, and speak your truth. Feel it move through your arms and hands, your palms flowing with energy—and the weight lifts off your shoulders.

Stand now, free of the weight, and feel the fire—the converted anger, the power that is your birthright as a man—move up through your head, your eyes brightening, your brow smoothing. Finally feel it burst out through the top of your head, the fire in your head making you fully alive and fully centered. You are no longer weighed down. You are no longer an imprisoned Titan; you are a man and you are in touch with your inner God—fully functional, fully alive.

SMUDGE RECIPE

Note: I have developed this smudge recipe over some time and its proportions vary, as do the amounts I make. I also cheerfully and freely admit it doesn't burn as well as straight sage, so I tend to burn it with a charcoal briquette of the kind used to burn loose incense. It has a floral overtone but a solid, manly undercurrent that I think works well for cleansing.

- 3 parts lavender flowers
- 2 parts crushed bay leaf
- 2 parts white sage
- 2 more parts, 1 part apiece, of any two of the following: cedar, sandalwood, chamomile, clove, cinnamon, myrrh, dragon's blood, or whatever you like

Crush anything larger than, say, a lavender leaf. (A food processor works well if you have one you and you can clean it very well, but there's something to be said for a plain old mortar and pestle. You can also borrow an idea from Alton Brown and use a small electric coffee grinder; just don't make coffee with it afterwards unless you like sage-cedar latte.)

Mix everything together, and leave the mixture out overnight to dry. Store it in a cloth bag that allows the mixture to breathe.

Good Smudge Pots

Because I use loose smudge, I tend to need something to burn it in. Here are a few ideas:

- A small, cast-iron skillet (idea courtesy of Fat Walrus from the Indiana ManKind Project community). I got mine at Goodwill for a couple of bucks. It holds heat incredibly well and has a handle. It's also almost impossible to break.

- A large shell. I've seen these used a lot. They do heat up, and there's no handle.

- Take a coffee can, punch two holes 180 degrees apart on the rim, and run a wire loop through them so you have a handle. Congratulations: you have a homemade thurible (a device you can swing back and forth to spread around incense or smudge fumes, as any former altar boy would know). This is great for smudging large groups of people. (This idea is courtesy of Great Bear from the Houston MKP community.)

- Any heavy, heatproof ceramic bowl. Again, Goodwill or thrift stores are your friends on this one. In fact, Goodwill is your friend for most ritual implements, but that's another book.

- Large metal incense burners designed to handle loose incense. After all, there isn't much real difference between loose or powdered incense and loose smudge.

Smudge Blessing

Repeat this while lighting the smudge:

Earth, Air, Fire, Water, Spirit,
All meet here.
Let the smoke from the smudge rise up
And carry my tension and concerns away
Leaving me cleansed, refreshed, and renewed.
So mote it be.

Cleansing Cloths

To give credit where credit is due, I first saw this used at the 2005 ManKind Project Elder Gathering in Bedford, Indiana, and I thought it was amazing.

Materials needed:

- A large baking dish. The foil pans sold as disposable roasting pans work really well.

- A large strainer. A metal mesh one works better than a plastic colander.

- As many clean dishtowels or hand towels as you expect to have men in the ritual, plus a few more for the guy who you didn't expect to show up.

- One larger, heavy towel, large enough to cover the pan completely.

- A large soup or stock pot.

- Several mixed citrus fruits. They can even be a bit bruised, since you won't be eating them. This is a good time to reduce, reuse, recycle, and reclaim your fruit drawer.

- Aromatic spices or herbs that go well together. I like clove, cinnamon, allspice, and a touch of musk—or, alternately, a strong infusion of lavender and sage. While I've never tried it, I'll bet that a mixture of mint and eucalyptus would work, too.

- A small cloth steeping bag of the kind used for herbal tea.

Roll each towel very tightly into a rat-tail. (Do not smack your friends on the butt with them. We're being mature here.)

Lay the towels closely together in the baking dish. They should touch each other and leave as little open space as possible.

Put the water on to boil. While it's heating, cut the citrus fruit into slices. Crush the herbs and spices if necessary and put them in the cloth steeping bag. When the water is boiling, lower the heat to a simmer and add in the citrus fruit and the herbs.

Let the mixture steep for a good long time until it is very aromatic. About twenty minutes before you expect to need the towels, pour the aromatic mixture (it should still be very warm) through a strainer onto the towels, soaking them through. Do not get them so wet that they unroll and float, but you want them to be saturated with the mixture.

Place the larger towel over the pan to hold in the steam and fragrance.

Offer the lightly wrung-out towels to men after any difficult ritual or other experience for cleansing, relaxing, and psychic rejuvenation.

There are obviously other aromatic combinations to be used in this process; I leave those up to those who are better versed in aromatherapy than I am.

CALLING THE DIRECTIONS

Formal

East: I call you, elders and spirits of the East. The colors are the rose of sunrise, yellow of morning, the gray of the mist of dawn. This is the direction of Air, of the Divine Child, the Youth, the Lover, the man beginning his road. Hail and welcome, spirits of the East!

South: I call you, elders and spirits of the South. The colors are the red of blood, the orange of fire, the silver of steel. This is the direction of Fire, of the Warrior, the Craftsman, the Challenger, the man at the height of his power. Hail and welcome, spirits of the South!

West: I call you, elders and spirits of the West. The colors are the blue of twilight, the black of shadows and mysteries, the slate gray-blue of the sea. This is the direction of Water, of the Magician, the Sacrificed One, the Trickster-shaman, the man with the knowledge and compassion to find out the truth. Hail and welcome, spirits of the West!

North: I call you, elders and spirits of the North. The colors are the green and brown of Earth, the gray of stone, the white of frost and snow. This is the direction of Earth, of the Elder, the King, the Guide, the man at the height of his wisdom and elder grace. Hail and welcome, spirits of the North!

Soul: I call you, elders and spirits of the Spirit and Soul. The colors are the gold of the inner power of men and the purple of the spirit. This is the direction of the Self, the Axis Mundi, the place where all the other directions meet. Hail and welcome, spirits of the Spirit and Soul!

Informal

> **Youth:** I call to the East, the spirits of Air! At the beginning of the day, we honor the beginning of the road, the morning from which life springs. Hail and welcome, spirits of the East, essence of Air!

> **Warrior:** I call to the South, the spirits of Fire! At the noontide of the day, we honor the heart of the road, the bright moment in which we are strongest, fastest, fleetest, best. Hail and welcome, spirits of the South, essence of Fire!

> **King:** I call to the West, the spirits of Water! At the end of the day, we honor the winding down of the road, the twilight in which we first begin to experience the unknown. Hail and welcome, spirits of the West, essence of Water!

> **Elder:** I call to the North, the spirits of Earth! In the heart of the night, we honor the end of the road, the dark midnight in which we finish our quest and begin the spiral anew. Hail and welcome, spirits of the North, essence of Earth!

Poetic

These quarter calls use the four primary archetypes from Robert Moore and Douglas Gillette.

> **Youth:** *In the morning's light, I stand here*
> *With all my brothers in this circle*
> *Honoring our inner Lover.*

> See the gold of spirit's sunrise,
> Feel the touch of animal spirits,
> Eagle, squirrel, butterfly, owl.
> Hail and welcome, O Air spirits!

Warrior: *Here I stand, in noontime's fire.*
> With all my brothers in this circle
> Honoring our inner Warrior.
> See the red of blood and fire
> Feel the touch of animal spirits—
> Lion, mouse, iguana, badger.
> Hail and welcome, Fire spirits!

Magician: *I stand alone in twilight's shadow.*
> With all my brothers in this circle
> Honoring our inner Wizard.
> See the blue of dusk and Water
> Feel the touch of animal spirits—
> Dolphin, otter, seagull, gator.
> Hail and welcome, Water spirits!

Sovereign: *I stand enthroned in Earth's embrace*
> With all my brothers in this circle
> Honoring our inner ruler.
> See the green of Mother Earth
> Feel the touch of animal spirits—
> Bison, grizzly, snake, and dragon.
> Hail and welcome, O Earth spirits!

FOR FURTHER THOUGHT

Books

Men's Spirituality

Moore, Robert, and Douglas Gillette. *King, Warrior, Magician, Lover: Rediscovering the Archetypes of the Mature Masculine*. San Francisco: HarperSanFrancisco, 1991.

This is really one of the primary sources for looking at men as archetypes, and it's one of my favorites. I refer back to it time and again.

Kipnis, Aaron R. *Knights Without Armor: A Guide to the Inner Lives of Men*. New York: Tarcher, 1991.

Another wonderful book and a great guide for the mature masculine. I have not had the privilege yet to read the 2004 revision and new edition, but I suspect it makes a good book even better.

Kauth, Bill. *A Circle of Men: The Original Manual for Men's Support Groups*. New York: St. Martin's Press, 1992.

The practical guide to setting up a men's group, this book is required reading for anyone interested in this work. Bill helped found the New Warrior Training Adventure.

Keen, Sam. *Fire in the Belly: On Being a Man*. New York: Bantam, 1992.

It's been a while since I read this, but it's a good resource. Keen makes some uncomfortable points—his emphatic rejection of "bondage to women" is pretty harsh—but it's still worth reading.

Bly, Robert. *Iron John: A Book about Men*. Cambridge, MA: Da Capo, 2004.

The original. Bly's work is the foundation of the mythopoetic movement, interpreting men's spiritualities in strong mythic and symbolic language. The best.

Briggs, Joe Bob. *Iron Joe Bob.* New York: Atlantic Monthly Press, 1993.

This great satire makes points about its subject that are worth taking in. Texas humorist and movie aficionado Briggs wrote Iron Joe Bob as a parody of the men's movement, and along the way makes some serious, important, and thought-provoking points about men, psychology, and society. One of my favorite books.

Paganism

Starhawk. *The Spiral Dance.* New York: HarperOne, 1999 (revised edition).

Starhawk's groundbreaking work made American neo-Paganism—and especially Eclectic Wicca—what it is today.

Gillotte, Galen. *Book of Hours: Prayers to the God.* St. Paul, MN: Llewellyn, 2002.

Gillotte is a poet and a bard, and these are some wonderful, heartfelt, and awe-inspiring prayers to various faces of the God. The single book I use the most in personal prayer.

Serith, Ceisiwr. *A Book of Pagan Prayer.* Newburyport, MA: Weiser, 2002.

Serith's groundbreaking work provides prayers for all uses, seasons, occasions, and has some wonderful prayers to the God.

Hutton, Ronald. *The Triumph of the Moon: A History of Modern Pagan Withcraft.* New York: Oxford University Press, 2001.

The authoritative history on the early days of Wicca. I mention it here not just because it's a great, great book—but because it subtly documents how many of the formative influences on early neo-Paganism and how many of the early neo-Pagans themselves were men.

Reed, Ellen Cannon. *Circle of Isis: Ancient Egyptian Magic for Modern Witches.* Franklin Lakes, NJ: New Page Books, 2002.

I can't count how many times I've referred to this book. It's the best work on using Egyptian deities in a Wiccan framework, but it's also the first book I've ever read that allowed for the concept that we could get new messages from old deities.

Harrington, David, and deTraci Regula. *Whispers of the Moon: The Life and Work of Scott Cunningham.* St. Paul, MN: Llewellyn, 1997.

The biography of one of the formative thinkers in eclectic Wicca, Whispers *is a living testament to a man who knew his archetypes and his gods.*

Bonewits, Isaac. *Real Magic; The Pagan Man; Bonewits's Essential Guide to Witchcraft and Wicca;* and, oh, anything else he's ever written.

Isaac Bonewits is the Smartest Man In Paganism. His works are invariably solid, and the three above are particularly brilliant.

Fisher, Amber Laine. *Philosophy of Wicca.* Toronto: ECW Press, 2002.

One of the best and most mature expressions of Wiccan and neo-Pagan philosophy and theology. Refreshingly free of spellwork and magick, this is not a grimoire but a work of serious and passionate religion.

Cunningham, Scott. *Living Wicca: A Further Guide for the Solitary Practitioner* (1993) and *Wicca: A Guide for the Solitary Practitioner* (1988). St. Paul, MN: Llewellyn.

Brilliant, groundbreaking works, and they've aged very well.

Kondratiev, Alexei. *The Apple Branch: A Path to Celtic Ritual.* New York: Citadel, 2003.

Krasskova, Galina. *Exploring the Northern Tradition.* Franklin Lakes, NJ: New Page Books, 2005.

My two favorite books on Celtic Reconstructuralism—better known as Druidry—and Norse Reconstructuralism, or Ásatrú.

Websites

Pagan

www.witchvox.com—The Witches' Voice

The greatest Pagan website in existence.

www.paganpride.org—The Pagan Pride Project

I admit to a certain bias, but I'm proud of the work we've done.

www.religioustolerance.org—Ontario Consultants on Religious Tolerance

One of the oldest resources on the Web, I remember using this site's resources ten years ago—an eon ago in Internet time. It's still one of the best pure resources for religious info on the Web, and their Pagan section is excellent.

www.aren.org—AREN (Alternative Religions Education Network)

I hate the term "alternative religion." My religion is not an alternative to anything, save perhaps ignorance. But AREN does great work, and it's work right in the trenches where it really counts.

www.circlesanctuary.org—Circle Sanctuary

For over thirty years, Selena Fox and Circle have been working tirelessly for Pagan rights and causes. Their subsidiary, the Lady Liberty League, regularly takes on those who discriminate against Pagans.

Men's

www.mkp.org—The website for the ManKind Project

I've talked enough of how wonderful this program is; it saved my life.

www.fathers4kids.com/html/home.htm—The National Fathers' Resource Center

A great resource for fathers' rights and resources.

www.menstuff.org—The National Men's Resource

If there is a comprehensive men's resource on the Web, this is it. More data than any three scholar deities could use.

I wish there were a good website for Pagan men's resources. Maybe that's next year's project.

APPENDIX II

CONVERTING SACRED PATH RITUALS TO SOLITARY WORK

I want to state something up front: I am one of the worst people I can imagine to write this section.

The fact is, I've never *been* a solitary Pagan practitioner. I have always been involved with a group of some size. In fact, the period of time from December 2005 to August 2006, after I moved from Indiana to Texas, was the longest I had gone without regular group ritual since 1991. My experience in writing rituals for solitaries is very close to nil.

In addition, I think that men's work is very dependent on working in a group. Men need other men to bounce ideas off of, to give honest feedback with an edge, and to help support each other as we work. While I try not to make gender distinctions, in my experience men are "pack animals"; we need other men around to struggle against and to catalyze our own internal processes.

So when it comes to modifying the group rituals in *Sacred Paths for Modern Men*, I am a little nonplussed. Nevertheless, I'm going to try to work out some guidelines for you to follow if you are either trying to do this work by yourself or with a small group of men that does not include all the ritual elements and ages I've described in the group rituals.

1. Don't sweat the small stuff

I said this before, but I'll say it again: in a perfect world, we would all have big ornate temples or hand-crafted lodges with lots of neat ritual accoutrements and shake-the-windows sound systems. Needless to say, this is not a perfect world—we have bills to pay, jobs to go to, responsibilities to take care of, and things that may need money spent on them long before you get to have that absolutely perfect wall tapestry or altar cloth.

Religious rituals are not like baking. You can—and in the case of this book are encouraged to—substitute. If you don't have something I call for, use something else. I will not hunt you down and smack you.

2. If you don't have the substance, have the spirit

Let's say, for example, that you have a great group of men to work with—but none of them are over forty. The fact that I've written these rituals with Elder roles and Elder energy does not mean that a group without an Elder can't perform them.

The Elder is about spiritual safety, psychic safety, and grounding. He takes care of the men in each ritual and provides that level of wisdom and even centering that makes group work with men effective. Simply find a man who can step into that role, and have him do the part of the Elder. The same applies for any other role: the energy of the King, the Magician, the Lover, and the Youth should all be readily obvious from their individual chapters, and that energy can be stepped into even if the age is wrong. Being in the right stage of life for these rituals helps, but it's not required.

As a solitary, your best friend may be aids or magickal tools. Each role in the ritual could have a colored stole, a mask, a ritual tool, or whatever item works for you to trigger you into the right energy stage.

The exception to this is the Eldering ritual at the end of chapter XII. I would reserve that for a man who has reached the proper age as well as the proper interest in that kind of work.

Here is a possible set of correspondences for symbols for men's work. Note that these are mine; yours may vary. While these symbols and correspondences have some basis in tradition and mythology, they are more an attempt to infuse these archetypes with consistent, modern, and personal meaning.

Archetype	Color	Tool	Animal	Incense
The Child	Gold	Ball	Butterfly	Lilac
The Lover	Rose	Cup	Swan	Rose
The Warrior	Red	Sword	Ram	Dragon's blood
The Trickster	Orange	Rattle	Monkey	Copal
The Green Man	Green	Smudge	Stag	Pine
The Guide	Tan	Staff	Owl	Frankincense
The Craftsman	Brown	Hammer	Beaver	Cedar
The Destroyer	Black	Axe	Panther	Myrrh
The Magician	Silver	Wand	Bear	Sandalwood
The King/Elder	Purple	Crown	Lion	Jasmine
The Healer	White	Crystal	Pelican	Nag Champa
The Sacrificed One	Blue	Seed	Phoenix	Amber

3. Find the right tools

Someday I'm going to write a whole book on this, but for now here's a simple rule I call the Thrift Store Principle: *you can find more useful ritual tools and altar trappings at the Salvation Army or Goodwill than you can at the mall.*

In the first appendix, I talked about various smudge tools—and I included such traditional magickal ephemera as the tin bucket and the cast-iron skillet. This principle of pragmatic magick (that'd make an interesting book title) can be applied to other traditional tools as well. Cauldron? Dutch oven. Athame? Oyster knife. Wand? Laser pointer or walking stick. Altar cloth? Remnants are cheap at your local MegaMart, and are often brightly colored for seasonal work. You do not need the fancy-schmancy $525 embroidered hand-spun Peruvian llama wool and crystal-thread ritual cloth from expen$ivenewagecrap.com. If you want to have it, that's one thing, but it's not required. Magick requires nothing but the will, the mind, and the heart. Everything else is theatre.

4. When in doubt, check other sources

What I know about solitary work you could put in a thimble. What Scott Cunningham knew you couldn't fit in an Olympic swimming pool. Do not, under any circumstances, consider any book—especially mine—to be the be-all and end-all of men's work. I encourage you to check other sources, take wisdom from them, and convert my rituals on the fly if necessary.

5. Finally, ask other men and be open to grace

You may read this and not be able to think of any other men who might like to do this work with you. Be aware you may be overlooking a man who needs you. I once had a very wise teacher—thanks, Mac—who told me we were all throwing ropes to the drowning, and when we pulled someone else in from the mess they were in we handed them a rope and set them to work on the beach. Asking a man if he wants to do this work with you, even if you're not sure he'll say yes, could be the step he needs to accomplish something great.

Remember Joe.
His name's actually not Joe,
Not probably. Perhaps it's Abraham,
Or Carlos, or Rajiv,
Or Amos, or Mohammed,
Or Steve, or Brandon.
But for the sake of brevity,
He's Joe, at least for now.

You probably know Joe.
Joe's the guy next door, next cubicle, next seat over at your house of worship.
You've probably talked with Joe, joked with him,
Talked sports or business.
I know I have.
Our days are filled with Joes.

What you don't know is that Joe's drowning.
He's afraid, he's hurt, he has old wounds.
He can't relate to his wife, his children, his lover.
He's out of a closet and defensive,
Or in a closet and terrified.
He can't talk about his feelings.
He can't show his feelings.
So he drowns his feelings

In anger, or alcohol, or drugs, or food, or any one of a
dozen other panaceas.
But they don't stop the pain; they only pause it.

Every man I see is Joe.
Every man I speak to is Joe.
I am an initiated warrior,
A man who has passed the first of a lifetime of gauntlets.
I am not in any way a complete work
But I'm closer than I was.
And I may be the only way that Joe finds out
He doesn't have to drown.
I may be Joe's life preserver, a rope thrown in a storm.
When I find myself caught up
In politics, in structure, in illusion
In my own shadow's web of self-importance
When I am out of mission and out of integrity
I have but one talisman against such enchantments.
I remember Joe.
Joe's waiting for me.
Joe's waiting for you.
Remember Joe.

About the Author

Dagonet Dewr has been one of the driving forces behind the Pagan Pride Project since its inception, currently serving as its executive director. He is also the past managing editor of *newWitch* magazine and an initiated warrior in the ManKind Project. He lives in Austin, Texas, with his wife Elisabeth and his children.